To my children,
Palma and David
P.B.

In memory of my in-laws,
Margaret, Zoltan, and Robert Hirschfeld
B.H.

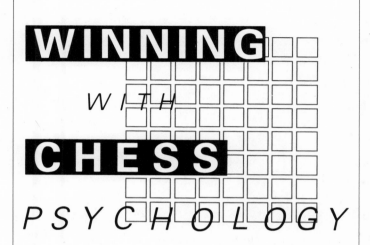

WINNING WITH CHESS PSYCHOLOGY

Pal Benko

and

Burt Hochberg

DAVID McKAY
COMPANY, INC.

Library of Congress Cataloging-in-Publication Data

Benko, Pal, 1928–
　　Winning with chess psychology / by Pal Benko and Burt
　　Hochberg.
　　p.　　cm.
　　ISBN 0-8129-1866-5
　　1. Chess—Psychological aspects. I. Hochberg, Burt. II.
　　Title.
　GV1448.B46　1991
　794.1'01'9—dc20　　　　　　　　　　　　　　90-22887

Designed by M 'N O Production Services, Inc.

Chess diagrams by M-Mate-Chess

Manufactured in the United States of America

9　8　7　6　5　4　3　2　1

First Edition

CONTENTS

PREFACE

The highest art of the chess player lies in
not allowing your opponent to show you
what he can do.
                    —World Champion Gary Kasparov

Is it better to play the board or the opponent?

Playing the board means choosing plans based
strictly on the objective characteristics of the position. Many great players of the past have played that
way, and many modern masters play that way today.
How could it be wrong?

Just before the turn of this century, World Champion Emanuel Lasker published a book, *Common
Sense in Chess*, in which he propounded a new philosophy of chess. He argued that chess was neither a
game nor a science nor an art, as had been thought at
various times in its long history, but a fight.

There can be but one objective in a fight, Lasker
wrote: winning. What does it matter, in the heat of
battle, whether or not a plan is theoretically sound?
Simply put, if it works, it's good; if it doesn't, it isn't.

Chess is played by human beings, Lasker empha-
sized, and to disregard their human frailties—that is,

to play the board—is to close one's eyes to a world of winning opportunities. To play with common sense means not only to choose plans according to the characteristics of the position—that goes without saying—but also with due regard for the characteristics of the *opponent.* "Chess is a fight in which all possible factors must be made use of," he asserted; *"a knowledge of the opponent's good and bad qualities is of the greatest importance."*

That sounds perfectly reasonable to us today. The idea of "psyching out" an opponent or rival, or "doing a number on his head," is familiar in all forms of competition, from the playing field to the boardroom. But it was a revolutionary concept in Lasker's time, and not everyone agreed with him.

Even today there are players—though not at the highest levels—who would choose the same plan in the same position no matter who the opponent or what the circumstances. There is much to be said for finding the objective "truth" in a position, the objectively "best" move. The trouble is: given two identical positions, the move that is best against player A in the first round of a tournament may not be best against player B in the last round. Once you accept the logic of this argument, as you must, you are ready to appreciate the often decisive role that psychological factors play in chess.

Psychology has become a standard weapon in the armory of modern chess. It is not unfair or unsporting or unethical or illegal or against the rules. It is simply the application of the principle, first enunciated by Lasker, that the best move is the one that disturbs the opponent the most.

Lasker, who was world champion for a record twenty-seven years, believed that players who understood human psychology should have an advantage over those who did not, other factors being equal. In this book we will show you how to obtain that advantage.

The book is divided into two parts. The first five chapters outline the development of the psychological method as practiced by its leading exponents of the past: Lasker, Alekhine, Botvinnik, and others. The rest of the book will show you, regardless of your playing strength, how to use in your own games what those and other great masters have taught by example. The purpose of this book is to make you a stronger player and to help you win more games.

■ ■ ■

WINNING WITH
CHESS
PSYCHOLOGY

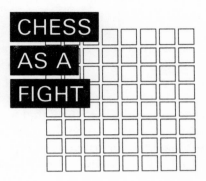

CHAPTER 1

CHESS AS A FIGHT

A typical chess game of a hundred years ago was like a medieval jousting contest: brutal and direct. Both sides, intent on straightforward attack against the enemy king, generally galloped toward each other with lances bent. The possible endgames that could result from a given strategy were hardly considered. All that mattered was checkmate.

Manly pride played an important role in this philosophy of the game. When a player offered a speculative sacrifice on the chessboard, he was throwing down the gauntlet, challenging his opponent to a duel; it could not honorably be declined. When a player attacked, he attacked the king; he would no sooner bend down to pick up a loose pawn than he would joust with a child.

Toward the end of the nineteenth century, many leading players began to see the tradition of manly honor in chess as foolish and self-destructive. Prudence and pragmatism began to supplant bravado. This new attitude was personified by an arrogant, cantankerous neurotic from Prague named Wilhelm Steinitz.

Steinitz believed that the choice of a plan or move must be based not on a single-minded desire for checkmate but on the objective characteristics of the position. One was not being a sissy to decline a sacrifice, he declared, if concrete analysis showed that accepting it would be dangerous. There was no shame in taking the trouble to win a pawn. A superior endgame was no less legitimate a goal of an opening or middlegame plan than was the possibility of a mating attack.

It wasn't long before Steinitz's successes forced other masters to revise their own approach to the game. They worked out more subtle methods of preparing and conducting an attack, and improved their defensive technique. Chess became more scientific, more "positional."

Soon after losing a telegraph match to that great Russian master of the attack, Mikhail Chigorin, Steinitz criticized his vanquisher's style as old-fashioned:

My opponent conducts his attack in the same manner as most of my match opponents, that is, as a representative of the old school. He is convinced that advancing pawns, even sacrificing a few, is useful for the purpose of creating difficulties on the kingside or to cramp the enemy pieces. I emphasize: the king is a strong piece, and in many cases he is capable of defending himself.

Chigorin scoffed at his rival's dogmatic theorizing:

Because I do not belong to any school, it is not the relative values of the pieces that determine my play, but only the

4

specific possibilities which I can analyze in detail. Each of my moves is determined by a figuring of variations; for this, general principles are of little value.

Although they differed, both men saw chess as a cold science: Steinitz claimed that it was governed by theoretical principles that needed only to be discovered, Chigorin that it yielded to brute-force calculation. Neither man showed the slightest awareness that sitting across the board was a human being.

Several generations later, World Champion Mikhail Botvinnik would have this to say about his Russian predecessor: "Chigorin's great weakness was that he did not always take his opponent's psychology into account; he was not sufficiently interested in the psychological factor in chess contests."

Botvinnik might also have described Steinitz in exactly those words, for Steinitz himself made his attitude perfectly plain: "I am fully and entirely concentrated on the board. I never even consider my opponent's personality. So far as I am concerned my opponent might as well be an abstraction or an automaton."

That statement was a product of 1894, the year in which Steinitz lost the world championship to a twenty-six-year-old master from Germany named Emanuel Lasker.

In 1896 Lasker published his first book, *Common Sense in Chess*. There we find this striking passage:

Chess has been represented, or shall I say misrepresented, as a game—that is, a thing which could not well serve a serious purpose, solely created for the enjoyment of an empty hour. If it were a game only, chess would never have survived the serious trials to which it has, during the long time of its existence, been often subjected. By some ardent enthusiasts chess has been elevated into a science or an art. It is neither; but its principle characteristic seems to be—what human nature mostly delights in—a fight. Not a fight, indeed, such as would tickle the nerves of coarser natures, where blood flows and the blows delivered leave their visible traces on the bodies of the combatants, but a fight in which the artistic, the purely intellectual element holds undivided sway.

This was the first expression of Lasker's theory of chess as a fight, a theory that would eventually revolutionize chess thinking.

Lasker was then twenty-eight. Two years earlier, at the time of his first match with Steinitz, he was practically unknown. He had earned his master's title only three years before and had achieved only one significant tournament success (at New York 1893, where he won all thirteen of his games). Though expected to fail miserably against his illustrious rival, he succeeded magnificently, winning ten games and losing five, with four draws.

During the next twenty-nine years, Lasker played in twelve tournaments; he came first in eight, tied for first in another, was second once, and tied for second once. In the same period he won matches against Steinitz (a rematch), Frank Marshall, Siegbert Tarrasch (twice), David Janowski, and others. He held the world championship uninterruptedly for twenty-seven years, a record that almost certainly will never be equaled.

After a nine-year hiatus between 1925 and 1934 (he had lost the world title to Capablanca in 1921),

Lasker returned to tournament chess at the age of sixty-five. In his first "comeback" tournament, Zurich 1934, he placed "only" fifth in a strong field of sixteen. A little more than a year later, in competition with the world's eighteen best players at the great Moscow tournament of 1935, Lasker, then sixty-seven years old, came in third without losing a game, a performance that was called a "biological miracle."

From his biographers and from his own writings we know that Lasker was never a student of the openings and that his technical preparation for tournaments was perfunctory, at best. Yet throughout his long career he was able to overcome opponents who were far better prepared, much younger, or both, and he often won even after obtaining inferior positions. How did he do it?

Savielly Tartakower, a significant player and theoretician and in his day a popular writer on the game, summed it up in 1929, on the occasion of Lasker's sixtieth birthday. Lasker, he wrote, "was the first to demonstrate in chess not only a brilliant combination (Morphy!) or a methodical system (Steinitz), but (and chiefly!) a knowledge of the opponent's personality, his weak and strong points, as an important element in obtaining victory."

Lasker himself had made that clear in 1924. A reporter for a Dutch newspaper had said to him, "I have heard that often you have carefully studied some of your opponent's games, you know both his weaknesses and his strong points."

"That is self-understood," Lasker replied, "and is entirely in line with my theoretical conception of the fight. A chess game, after all, is a fight in which all possible factors must be made use of, and in which a knowledge of the opponent's good and bad qualities is of the greatest importance."

A vivid example is the following game, in which Lasker almost contemptuously exploits his opponent's well-known predilection for attack.

MATCH, 1907
Ruy Lopez

F. Marshall	Em. Lasker
1 e4	e5
2 Nf3	Nc6
3 Bb5	Nf6
4 d4	exd4
5 0-0	Be7
6 e5	Ne4
7 Nxd4	0-0
8 Nf5	d5
9 Bxc6	bxc6
10 Nxe7 +	Qxe7
11 Re1	Qh4

Thus far Lasker has declined his opponent's offers of gambit pawns (moves 5-8). Frank Marshall, an American virtuoso of the kingside attack, was at the time of this game thirty years old and at the peak of his considerable powers. His reputation, though it intimidated many of his opponents, worked to his disadvantage against Lasker, who now starts an attack and forces Marshall into the unaccustomed and uncomfortable role of defender.

Objectively the best move for Black is 11 . . . f6. The aggressive text move is not unsound, however, and considering its effect on Marshall, perhaps it, not 11 . . . f6, should be considered "objectively the best move" against this specific opponent.

12 Be3	f6
13 f3	

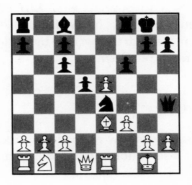

13 ...	fxe5(!)

Though this piece sacrifice is not a mistake, neither should it lead to an advantage for Black. But against Marshall it is the right decision because it forces the great attacker to defend.

14 fxe4	d4

Thus Black recovers his sacrificed piece: if 15 Bd2 Bg4! 16 Qc1 Rf2! should win for Black.

A positional player like Tarrasch (as Tarrasch himself wrote in his analysis of this game) would now avoid complications by giving back the piece with 15 Qe2, hoping eventually to exploit Black's weaknesses on the queenside. But an aggressive player like Marshall was not one to avoid complications—which is precisely what Lasker was counting on when he started his attack.

| 15 g3 | Qf6 |
| 16 Bxd4 | |

A better try is 16 Bd2 Qf2+ 17 Kh1 Bh3 18 Rg1. Tarrasch then gives 18 ... h5 19 Na3 Bg4 20 Rf1! with drawing chances. Tartakower's suggestion, 18 ... Bf1!?, looks more promising.

| 16 ... | exd4 |
| 17 Rf1 | |

Due to his seriously weakened kingside, Marshall cannot hope for salvation in the middlegame but must take his chances in the endgame.

17 ...	Qxf1+
18 Qxf1	Rxf1+
19 Kxf1	Rb8!
20 b3	Rb5

21 c4

Richard Reti, marveling at the clever strategy by which Lasker has managed to obtain a passed pawn, gives the variation 21 Nd2 Rh5 22 Kg2 Rc5 23 Rcl Ba6 threatening . . . Bd3 with great advantage for Black. "The fact that Black has refrained from making the obvious move 19 . . . Ba6 +," wrote Reti, ". . . has induced White to move 21 c4, thereby giving Black a passed d-pawn, which finally decides the issue."

The game concluded: 21 . . . Rh5 22 Kg1 c5 23 Nd2 Kf7 24 Rf1 + Ke7 25 a3 Rh6 26 h4 Ra6 27 Ra1 Bg4 28 Kf2 Ke6 29 a4 Ke5 30 Kg2 Rf6 31 Re1 d3 32 Rf1 Kd4 33 Rxf6 gxf6 34 Kf2 c6 35 a5 a6 36 Nf1 Kxe4 37 Ke1 Be2 38 Nd2 + Ke3 39 Nb1 f5 40 Nd2 h5 41 Nb1 Kf3 White resigned.

Lasker's great rival in the decade 1900–1910 was Dr. Siegbert Tarrasch. Dr. Tarrasch, a man of medicine, by inclination a scientist, was a disciple of Steinitz. The idea of reducing chess to absolute scientific formulas was as natural a way of thinking for Tarrasch as it was anathema for Lasker (though Lasker, too, admired Steinitz). The differences between the two men were clearly explained by Reti:

> The theory of Steinitz could be further developed in two directions. On the one hand it could be elaborated philosophically, as a general theory of the fight, for which chess offers a clear and definite example. On the other hand it could be developed purely from the viewpoint of practical chess with the idea of finding that form for the theory which would be most suitable for the practical execution of a chess game. Lasker followed the first lead which took him somewhat too far off the beaten path to win any immediate following, while Tarrasch chose the other way, thereby giving the theory of chess the beginning of a scientific form.

The two matches between Lasker and Tarrasch for the world championship were contests not only between two chess giants but also between two diametrically opposed theories of the game. On the eve of the first match, in 1908, Lasker set the stage:

> Dr. Tarrasch is a thinker, fond of deep and complex speculation. He will accept the efficacy and usefulness of a move if at the same time he considers it beautiful and theoretically right. But I accept that sort of beauty only if and when it happens to be useful. He admires an idea for its depth, I admire it for its efficacy. My opponent believes in beauty, I believe in strength. I think that by being strong a move is beautiful too.

The second game of that first match was called by Dr. Hannak, Lasker's biographer, "one of the most remarkable of Lasker's many demonstrations of 'psychological warfare' on the chess board." Noting that Tarrasch, in his own comments on this game, had called Lasker's fourteenth move "evidently an oversight," Hannak writes: "How little he knew his wily opponent! It was anything but an oversight, it was Lasker the psychologist at his best. The move put his opponent in the quandary of having to choose between winning a pawn immediately or continuing a promising attack. . . . Lasker was never in any doubt as to what that decision would be; he knew his opponent's mind rather better than Tarrasch did himself."

It is Black's move. He can do nothing constructive without creating weaknesses in his own position. Tarrasch, who loved to tie his opponents in knots, must have been happy. But, wrote Reti, "a game of chances and counterchances is much less in keeping with Tarrasch's style . . ." Lasker's next move, he continued, "which must be regarded as a blunder when

Em. Lasker

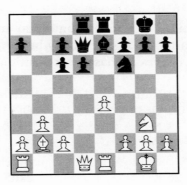

S. Tarrasch

viewed objectively, is psychologically altogether admirable."

| 14 ... | Ng4(!) |
| 15 Bxg7! | Nxf2! |

Of course, 15 ... Kxg7 is answered by 16 Nf5 + and 17 Qxg4.

16 Kxf2

Tarrasch cannot resist winning a pawn. How could it be wrong? A real attacking player would choose to keep the attack going with the better 16 Qd4, but Tarrasch prefers an extra pawn.

16 ...	Kxg7
17 Nf5 +	Kh8
18 Qd4 +	f6

| 19 Qxa7 | Bf8 |
| 20 Qd4 | Re5! |

Black is building strong counterplay in the center, but White still stands objectively better. Amazingly, in ten moves Tarrasch has a lost position!

21 Rad1	Rde8
22 Qc3	Qf7
23 Ng3	Bh6
24 Qf3	d5
25 exd5	Be3 +
26 Kf1	cxd5
27 Rd3	Qe6
28 Re2	f5
29 Rd1	f4
30 Nh1	d4
31 Nf2	Qa6!
32 Nd3	Rg5
33 Ra1	Qh6!

White can't save his h-pawn: if 34 h3 Rg3 35 Qd5 f3.

34 Ke1	Qxh2
35 Kd1	Qg1 +
36 Ne1	Rge5
37 Qc6	R5e6
38 Qxc7	R8e7
39 Qd8 +	Kg7
40 a4	f3!
41 gxf3	Bg5
White resigned	

"I am thoroughly ashamed of that game," Tarrasch moaned. He always considered this loss to have been a result of Lasker's "incredible luck."

It's a well-known axiom of sport, however, that the great player is always lucky. It often happens that a player who has had an advantage during the game but ended up losing blames his loss on bad luck. The true culprit, however, is bad psychology. In his *Manual of Chess* Lasker writes that loss generally occurs "when the player overrates his advantage or for other reasons seeks to derive from a minute advantage a great return such as a forced win."

An example is his "lucky" win against Schiffers at Nuremberg 1896.

E. Schiffers

Em. Lasker

Lasker, with the white pieces, is a few pawns down, but he can practically force a draw by perpetual check with 28 Ne7+ Kb8 29 Nc6+, etc. Objectively, that would have been the correct course. But his knowledge of human nature—or of Schiffers specifically—led him to suspect that his opponent would get careless or complacent with his "winning" material advantage.

28 Rxg7(!)	Kb8
29 Nxf6	b5
30 Rg5!	Bd3
31 Nd7+	Kc7
32 Ne5	Be4
33 f5	Ra2
34 f6	Ra8
35 f7	Kd6
36 Rg8	Ke7
37 Kf4	Bd5
38 Rg7	Rh8

Instead, either 38 . . . b4 or 38 . . . Kf6 draws quickly.

39 Kg5	h6+?
40 Kf5	Be6+
41 Kg6	Rc8
42 Rh7	

42 . . .	h5(?)

Schiffers will not accept less than a full point, but since a full point is not justified by the position, he loses. His last chance to draw was 42 . . . Rf8.

16

Luck was again named the victor in this game, but in light of what we know about Lasker, it is clear that he deliberately steered for complications in order to disturb his opponent. Schiffers, as Lasker had hoped, was unable to make the difficult psychological adjustment when his "win" evaporated.

Now a "miracle" occurs: even with the little material remaining on the board, White gets a mating attack!

43 f8(Q) + !!	Kxf8
44 Kf6	Bg8
45 Re7!	Bh7
46 Rxh7	Kg8
47 Rg7 +	Kf8
48 Rb7	Ra8
49 Rf7 +	Ke8

Lasker announced mate in six—50 Re7+ Kd8 51 Nf7+ Kc8 52 Nd6+ Kd8 53 Ke6 Ra7 54 Rxa7 and 55 Rd7 mate—and Black resigned.

Lasker was often called lucky by those who failed to appreciate his theory that chess was a fight between two *personalities*. It was his understanding of human fallibility that led him, in 1926, to make the following remarkable assertion in his *Manual of Chess*:

He who has a slight disadvantage plays more attentively, inventively and more boldly than his antagonist who either takes it easy or aspires after too much. Thus a slight disadvantage is very frequently seen to convert into a good, solid advantage.

If Lasker truly believed that a slight disadvantage carried the seeds of a "good, solid advantage," could it be that he deliberately strove to obtain slightly disadvantageous positions? Richard Reti, in his great book *Masters of the Chessboard* (1933), suggested exactly that:

> In analyzing Lasker's tournament games I was struck by his lasting and at first seemingly incredible good luck. . . . Again and again I studied Lasker's games to discover the secret of his success. There is no denying the fact that over and over again Lasker's layout of the game is poor, that he is in a losing position a hundred times and nevertheless wins in the end. The hypothesis of lasting luck is too improbable. A man who steadily wins such success must be possessed of surprising power. But why then the bad, the losing positions? There is only one answer which may sound paradoxical at first blush: Lasker often deliberately plays badly.

With all due respect to Reti, who was usually an astute and sympathetic observer, it is simply impossible to accept the proposition that any master will deliberately play badly to obtain an inferior position in a serious game. Risky moves, yes; intentionally bad ones, never. What Reti perceived as a bad move was often one that Lasker, taking into account all the elements of the struggle, not least of them his opponent's personality, saw as his best *practical* chance. Lasker was not concerned with theoretical correctness but with pragmatic results. A good move was one that worked.

Although it is undeniable that Lasker often landed in inferior positions after the opening, that can be blamed as much on his superficial preparation as on his provocative methods. But having landed in an inferior position, and required to choose between a "correct" but passive plan and a risky but active one, Lasker always chose the latter.

An illustration is the following win against the man he most loved to beat, his arch-rival during his years as world champion, Dr. Tarrasch.

MÄHRISCH-OSTROW 1923
Alekhine's Defense

Em. Lasker	S. Tarrasch
1 e4	Nf6
2 e5	Nd5
3 c4	Nb6
4 d4	d6
5 f4	dxe5
6 fxe5	Nc6
7 Be3	Bf5
8 Nc3	e6
9 Nf3	Bb4
10 Bd3?	

This opening, having been introduced only a few years earlier, was not yet well known. Certainly Lasker had not analyzed it carefully, if at all. Here he makes the common mistake of allowing his king's knight to be pinned and exchanged. The correct move is 10 Be2, as the text continuation makes clear.

10 ...	Bg4
11 Be2	Bxf3
12 gxf3	Qh4 +
13 Bf2	Qf4

14 Rg1(!)

Lasker, already in an awkward position, takes immediate steps to create complications. This move costs a pawn, but to Lasker anything was preferable to passivity. Is this an example of how Lasker "deliberately played badly"? Suffice it to say that, as a consequence of this move, Tarrasch commits a strategic error on his twenty-fourth move that gives Lasker a winning position.

14 ...	0-0-0
15 Rg4	Qxh2
16 Rh4	Qg2
17 Bf1	Qg5
18 Qc2	h5
19 Rd1	Qh6
20 a3	Be7
21 Rh3	Bg5
22 Qe4	f6
23 exf6	Qxf6
24 Be2	Qf5?

Thus far Tarrasch has made no serious mistakes and has kept his extra pawn. Generally, it's a good idea to simplify by trading down when you have an extra pawn. Tarrasch, whose greatest weakness was his dogmatism, failed to realize, however, that in this particular position it was *not* a good idea. The reason is that after the exchange of queens Black's e-pawn is diverted from its important task of guarding d5. With that square entirely in White's hands, White's queenside pawns are mobilized, and they decide the game.

25 Qxf5	exf5
26 Bd3	g6
27 Ne2	h4
28 f4	Bf6
29 b4	Kb8
30 d5	Ne7
31 Kf1	Nbc8
32 b5	c6?

The decisive mistake, opening the b-file for White. Black should have tried to get his knight to e4, starting with 32 . . . Nd6.

The game concluded: 33 bxc6 bxc6 34 Rb1+ Ka8 35 Nd4 Bxd4 36 Bxd4 Rh7 37 Be5 Nd6 38 c5 Nb7 39 d6 Nd5 40 Rc1 Rf8 41 Ba6 Nf6 42 Bxf6 Rxf6 43 Re3 Rf8 44 Rce1 Rhh8 45 d7 Kb8 46 Re8+ Kc7 47 Bxb7 Black resigned.

"Lasker's opponent," wrote Reti, "never has a chance of playing a position which suits him. Objectively speaking, the opponent often stands a good chance of winning, but again and again he confronts problems that are new and especially difficult for him . . . The opponent's nervous collapse and shattered morale finally result in a catastrophe at the chess board."

This position, from a game played at Nuremberg

1896, is a good demonstration of Lasker the fighter at his best.

M. Chigorin

Em. Lasker

After playing the opening rather tamely, Lasker tried to force the game, got in trouble, and had to go into an endgame a pawn down. He now stands clearly worse, but, as always, he tries to make things as difficult as possible for his opponent.

33 Qe7   Qc2

33 ... Qc6 is better. Chigorin, a fierce attacking player, always liked to get his pieces as close as he could to the enemy king.

34 h4	a5
35 bxa5	bxa5
36 h5	a4
37 g4	Qc1

So as to meet 38 g5 with 38 . . . Qf4.

38 Kg3!!

Lasker, though a pawn down and with his opponent in possession of a distant passed pawn, calmly prepares an attack on Black's king. What effrontery!

Black should now be satisifed with 38 . . . a3 39 g5! hxg5 40 Nxg5 Qg1+ and perpetual check. If White tries 40 Qd8+ Ne8! 41 Qxe8+ Kh7 42 Qxf7, Black wins with 42 . . . Qf4+. But Chigorin, sensing no danger, plays out his "win."

38 . . .	g5?!
39 hxg6	fxg6
40 Qd8+	Kf7
41 g5!	h5
42 Qd7+	Kf8
43 Qxa4	h4+?

There may still have been a draw with 43 . . . Qb1 44 Qd7 Qf5. Chigorin, now realizing that he has been cheated of his win, cannot adjust mentally to the new situation and becomes confused.

44 Kg4	Qh1
45 Qd7	Qg2+
46 Kf4	Ne8
47 Qxe6	Qxf2
48 Qxg6	Qg3+
49 Ke3	Qg4
50 e6	Nd6
51 Qf6+	Ke8
52 Qh8+!	Ke7
53 Qg7+	Black resigned

An appreciation of Lasker by Tartakower includes this observation:

Lasker was always guided by his unswerving belief in the elasticity of the position. Only in this manner—and not by means of the usual fatuous explanations, such as individual style and will to win—can the universality of his chess creations be explained, a universality which enabled him for decades to steer clear of all schools, tendencies and imitations—only in the end to become the father of ultramodern chess.

Lasker's ideas, because they made the vital connection between chess and life, have become a permanent, essential part of the game. Many of the leading Soviet-trained players of our own era—Bronstein, Tal, Spassky, Korchnoi, to name just a few—acknowledge their debt to Lasker. Indeed, the "dynamic, intuitive" style of play promulgated by the Soviet school is nothing more than Lasker's philosophy of the struggle taken a step or two farther.

David Bronstein, in the introduction to his book on the 1953 Candidates tournament in Zurich (published in English as *The Chess Struggle in Practice*), writes:

Precisely this manner of conducting the struggle was characteristic of Emanuel Lasker's style, and, because it was not understood by any of his contemporaries, it was one of his main advantages. Lasker, the greatest psychologist in chess, did not have only this one trait, however. He knew how to swing the pendulum of the struggle back and forth as no one else did, not exceeding the bounds of safety himself but imperceptibly pushing his opponent toward the precipice.

In 1921, when Lasker was fifty-three, he lost the world championship to José Raúl Capablanca, a man twenty years his junior. Capablanca was quite invulnerable to Lasker's tactic of luring his opponents into murky complications where they were likely to make mistakes. For one thing, Capablanca very rarely made mistakes. For another, he didn't mind playing dull positions; he would rather draw than risk complications. (It is interesting to compare Lasker's career record of 30 percent draws with Capablanca's record of 43 percent. With the black pieces, Lasker's record was 31 percent, Capablanca's 48 percent.)

In defense of the psychological method, we should point out that Capablanca's purity of style and virtually errorless play was unique in the history of chess, and it remained so until Bobby Fischer's peak years half a century later. As Lasker showed, his methods worked against fallible human beings, not "machines" like Capablanca.

The only player who could have beaten Capablanca was Capablanca himself. And that is precisely what he did in 1927, when he lost the world title to another strong believer in the psychological method, an admirer of Lasker named Alexander Alekhine.

CHAPTER 2

■ ■ ■

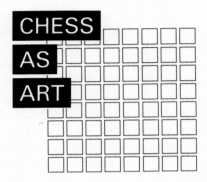

Lasker was a man of great intellect and many interests. In addition to chess and other games, he was fascinated by mathematics, philosophy, economics, and other subjects.

Alexander Alekhine, the scion of a noble Russian family, was a man of intellect and education, too, but for him chess was everything. It was at the center of his being, the only thing that mattered. Away from the chessboard his life was eccentric and unhappy. But when immersed in chess he was fulfilled, the master of his universe.

Alekhine was the outstanding representative of the psychological approach after Lasker, and he made no secret of his debt to the older man. "Emanuel Lasker has been my teacher all my life," he said in 1934, while he was world champion. "But for him I would not be what I am."

Alekhine once admitted, with commendable self-awareness, that for a long time he could not rid himself of the idea that he would always be able to find a way out of a difficult position. But as he matured, he realized that his innate talent for combinations was not enough to make him a world-class player. He therefore set up a strict regimen that would enable him to meet the great challenges that he knew lay ahead. He wrote:

I consider the three following factors essential for success. First, a realization of your own strong and weak points; second, an accurate knowledge of your opponent's strong and weak points; third, a higher objective than momentary satisfaction. I see this objective to be scientific and artistic achievements which place chess on a level with the other arts.

During the 1920s, Alekhine attempted repeatedly to arrange a match for the world championship against Capablanca, who had taken the title from Lasker in 1921. (In those days, before there was a world chess federation, the world titleholder alone decided how often he would defend his title and against whom.) When Capablanca finally agreed to play the match in 1927, Alekhine began meticulous preparations.

This match was a turning point in chess history, and not merely because the world championship changed hands. Alekhine's intense study of his opponent's style and personality elevated the importance of psychology in chess to an unprecedented level.

Alekhine reasoned first of all that in match play, as opposed to tournament play, a loss is extremely difficult to make up, for in a match there are no weak players from whom to get needed points. Therefore, he knew he would have to curb his inclination to create risky complications at every opportunity. A miscalculation at the wrong time could cost him not just a single game but conceivably the entire match.

Alekhine made an especially close study of the games the world champion had played in the New York tournament of 1927, just months before the match was to start. Capablanca's opening repertoire was limited, Alekhine found, but what he played he knew extremely well. Alekhine also noticed that the great Cuban had a tendency to simplify the position the moment he sensed danger. But many of the positions Capa had drawn were against lesser players, or contained weaknesses, or were seriously passive or defensive. All right then, Alekhine decided, let him simplify! If I don't crush him with my combinations, I'll outplay him.

The challenger's study of the champion's middlegame play was fruitful, too. Alekhine found that Capablanca's remarkable natural gifts sometimes lulled him into complacency or superficiality. Capa almost never blundered, but he was not immune to playing second-best moves.

And in the endgame, where Capablanca was reputed to be supreme, Alekhine found him to be uncreative. "Capablanca," he wrote years later, "was not a uniquely talented master of the endgame . . . his art in this phase of the game was characteristically technical."

And what was Capablanca doing while his challenger was preparing for the supreme test of his character and determination? Capa, obviously regarding the match as a routine matter, was keeping up his customary lifestyle of wine, women, and song. Why not? After all, Alekhine had never beaten him. Capablanca's cavalier attitude was a fatal psychological blunder that cost him the world championship.

"Psychology," Alekhine wrote after the match, "is the most important factor in chess. My success was due solely to my superiority in the sense of psychology. Capablanca played almost entirely by a marvelous gift of intuition, but he lacked the psychological sense."

Alekhine's triumph over Capablanca proved not only the correctness of his method of preparation but also the accuracy of his assessments of his own and his opponent's play. His penchant for combinations, which had been one of his hallmarks since puberty, was nowhere in evidence during this match. He won by exploiting the weaknesses he had discerned in his rival's play and by suppressing the risky tendencies in his own.

Alekhine's preparations paid off in the opening game of the match, his first win ever against Capablanca.

WORLD CHAMPIONSHIP, 1927
Game 1
French Defense

J. R. Capablanca	A. Alekhine
1 e4	e6
2 d4	d5
3 Nc3	Bb4
4 exd5	exd5
5 Bd3	Nc6
6 Ne2	Nge7
7 0-0	Bf5
8 Bxf5	Nxf5
9 Qd3	Qd7
10 Nd1	

It is typical of match strategy to play cautiously at first, but Capablanca's knight maneuvers allow

Alekhine to seize the initiative. The natural 10 Bf4
0-0-0 leads to a livelier game.

10 ...	0-0
11 Ne3	Nxe3
12 Bxe3	Rfe8
13 Nf4	Bd6!
14 Rfe1	

After 14 Nxd5 Bxh2+ 15 Kxh2 Qxd5 16 c4 Qh5+
17 Kg1 Rad8 18 d5 Ne5 Black has the initiative. 14 c3
is safer and avoids complications.

14 ...	Nb4
15 Qb3	

15 Qd2 is better, to protect the first rank, but Black
would still have the initiative after 15 . . . Qf5 16 Rec1
h5.

15 ...	Qf5
16 Rac1	

Another mistake, allowing a nice little combination
and fully confirming Alekhine's insight about Capablanca's superficial calculation. The right move is 16
Nd3, but even then, after 16 . . . Nxd3 17 Qxd3 Qxd3
18 cxd3 Black has the better endgame.

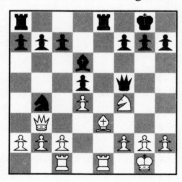

16 . . .	Nxc2!
17 Rxc2	Qxf4
18 g3	Qf5

Alekhine was tempted to play for attack with 18 . . . Qf3 19 Qxb7 h5 20 Qb5 h4 21 Qe2 Qf5, but he decided to stick to his planned match strategy of avoiding unnecessary complications.

19 Rce2	b6
20 Qb5	h5
21 h4	Re4
22 Bd2	

This temporary pawn sacrifice is the best chance.

22 . . .	Rxd4

The sacrifice need not be accepted, however. Simpler is 22 . . . Rae8 23 Qxe8+ Rxe8 24 Rxe8+ Kh7.

23 Bc3	Rd3
24 Be5	Rd8
25 Bxd6	Rxd6
26 Re5	Qf3
27 Rxh5	Qxh5
28 Re8+	Kh7
29 Qxd3+	Qg6
30 Qd1	Re6!

Alekhine returns the extra pawn in exchange for an aggressive position. Much less convincing is 30 . . . d4 31 Qf3 threatening 32 Qa8, and after 31 . . . c6 32 h5 Black has problems.

31 Ra8	Re5!
32 Rxa7	c5

33 Rd7	Qe6
34 Qd3+	g6
35 Rd8	d4
36 a4	Re1+

The attack on the king wins quickly. Black could also have trapped White's rook: 36 . . . Qe7! 37 Rb8 (*37 Qb3 Re6!*) 37 . . . Qc7 38 Ra8 Qb7, threatening both . . . Qxa8 and . . . Re1+.

37 Kg2	Qc6+
38 f3	Re3
39 Qd1	Qe6
40 g4	Re2+
41 Kh3	Qe3
42 Qh1	Qf4!
43 h5	Rf2

White resigned

Capablanca, tacitly admitting his unpreparedness to meet the French Defense, did not venture 1 e4 again in this match.

The champion got even by winning the third game, and then took the lead with a win in the seventh. But Alekhine, never losing faith in his match strategy, won games eleven and twelve and was once again in front.

Now a war of nerves was fought through nine straight draws. Capablanca, though one point behind, was content to test Alekhine's patience, hoping that the volatile challenger would revert to his natural risky style.

Capablanca was not at all wrong to adopt that strategy, considering the scoring conditions of the match. Alekhine had to win six games outright to take the title, but Capablanca would remain champion if the score reached 5-5. Draws did not count in the scoring. So although at this moment the score was 3-2 in Alekhine's favor, in a sense it was even: the title would go to whoever got the next three wins!

Alekhine, however, stuck to his plan: he avoided complications and even agreed to quick draws. With a one-game advantage, he had no need to rush matters but could bide his time and wait for a break.

It came in game twenty-one, when a slight inaccuracy by Capablanca gave Alekhine a brilliant win. Now Capa was two games behind, and although he stayed close by winning game twenty-five, he could no longer withstand the challenger's pressure. He lost games thirty-two and thirty-four, and Alekhine was the new world champion. "I have fulfilled my life's dream," Alekhine exulted, "and harvested the crop of my long years of striving."

As champion, Alekhine participated often in tournaments, winning many first prizes and proving beyond any doubt that he was worthy of the crown he wore. Public pressure and his constant need for money required him also to defend his title from time to time. This he did, but by choosing opponents who represented no real danger to him while managing to avoid a rematch with Capablanca. In two matches, in 1929 and 1934, he easily dispensed with Bogolyubov, who was clearly not in Alekhine's class, and in 1935 he prepared to meet another challenger he thought he could beat without too much trouble, Max Euwe. A popular figure in his native Holland, Euwe was a particularly attractive challenger because he had many wealthy supporters and could easily raise the large challenge purse demanded by the champion.

The match with Euwe turned out to be the most serious setback of Alekhine's career. In underestimating the big Dutchman, Alekhine made the same grave psychological blunder that Capablanca had made in 1927. His work habits were haphazard, he was in poor physical condition due to his heavy drinking (which he continued even during the match), and his technical preparation, especially in the openings, was superficial.

Alekhine was devastated by his loss. At the conclusion of the match, he asked for and was granted a rematch, to be played in 1937. This time he vowed to be ready. He pulled himself together and gave up both drinking and smoking. Nothing mattered now but his preparations for the rematch. Botvinnik, writing about this period of Alekhine's career, made a point of mentioning the change in Alekhine's psychological approach:

In his last period (1934–46) his play was characterized by a new, and one might say a Lasker-manner of approach to chess. During these years he did not so much attempt to penetrate into the secret of a position as to seek a convenient moment when without blundering he could shatter his opponent with the combinative weapon, even in positions where the prerequisites were lacking.

It is true that Alekhine's psychological approach changed in his last period (he died in 1946), but this happens to most masters. With maturity comes wisdom; with experience comes insight. In fact, they are the older player's main compensation for his younger opponents' greater energy and more reliable memory.

In the rematch with Euwe, Alekhine resorted to the combinative weapon with brilliant effect. After five games Euwe was leading by one point, but in the sixth, Alekhine delivered a staggering psychological shock that was felt throughout the match.

WORLD CHAMPIONSHIP, 1937
Game 6
Slav Defense

A. Alekhine	M. Euwe
1 d4	d5
2 c4	c6
3 Nc3	

In the first match the more common 3 Nf3 had been played here. But for this game Alekhine had something special up his sleeve.

3 . . .	dxc4
4 e4!	e5

The standard reply and the best. If 5 dxe5 Qxd1 + and 6 . . . Be6.

5 Bxc4?!

According to modern theory, 5 Nf3 exd4 6 Qxd4 is supposed to favor White slightly.

5 . . .	exd4

6 Nf3!?

In some published accounts of the match, Alekhine was suspected of being drunk, a story that fell on believing ears since he was known to have been drinking heavily during the first match. What else could explain such a highly speculative piece sacrifice on the sixth move of a title match against the world champion?

The sacrifice was not in fact an over-the-board inspiration but had been prepared well in advance. It placed Euwe under tremendous pressure, since he now had to spend a great deal of time calculating many difficult variations that Alekhine had earlier worked out at his leisure. Euwe's emotions must have been in turmoil, too, especially when his calculations told him that all the variations seemed to favor White!

It was his agitated emotional state—"sacrificial shock"—that caused Euwe to miss the one variation that refutes Alekhine's sacrifice: after 6 . . . dxc3 7 Bxf7+ Ke7 8 Qb3 cxb2 9 Bxb2 Qb6 10 Bxg8 Rxg8! 11 Qxg8 Qb4+ 12 Nd2 Qxb2 Black has a material advantage and his king is in no more danger than White's.

6 . . .   b5?

Euwe simply overlooked White's reply.

7 Nxb5!   Ba6

On 7 . . . cxb5 White wins the exchange with 8 Bd5.

8 Qb3!   Qe7

If 8 . . . Bxb5 9 Bxf7+ Kd7 10 Nxd4 (*10 Bxg8? Rxg8 11 Qxg8?? Bb4+*) with a tremendous attack.

The game didn't last much longer: 9 0-0 Bxb5 10

Bxb5 Nf6 11 Bc4 Nbd7 12 Nxd4 Rb8 13 Qc2 Qc5 14 Nf5 Ne5 15 Bf4 Nh5 16 Bxf7+ Kxf7 17 Qxc5 Bxc5 18 Bxe5 Rb5 19 Bd6 Bb6 20 b4 Rd8 21 Rad1 c5 22 bxc5 Bxc5 23 Rd5 and Black resigned. If 23 . . . Rc8 24 Bxc5 and 25 Nd6+.

This game not only equalized the score but was undoubtedly responsible for Euwe's losing the next two games. It's not easy to take a beating like this and the next day have to face the man who gave it to you.

The ninth game was drawn, but Euwe lost again in the tenth to another of Alekhine's combinative shock treatments.

M. Euwe

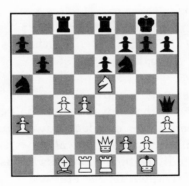

A. Alekhine

Black's position looks normal and safe. In positions like this, Black usually manages to work up some play against White's hanging pawns. But Alekhine has no intention of letting the game take such a mundane course.

23 g4!?

The threat is 24 Kg2 and 25 Nf3, trapping the queen. Notice that Black's knight cannot get out of the way to allow the queen to retreat. And 23 ... Qxh3 doesn't help because of 24 Rd3 Qh4 25 Kg2 and 26 Rh3 (or *26 Rh1*). Euwe, again faced with unexpected tactical problems, again misses the right answer.

23 ...   Nc6?

Necessary is 23 ... h6 24 Kg2 Nh7. Alekhine then suggests 25 d5 exd5 26 cxd5, pointing out that 26 ... f6 is not playable because 27 Nf3 Rxe2 28 Rxe2! wins the exchange. True, but Black can hold with 26 ... Nc4!.

24 Kg2!   Nxe5
25 dxe5   Nh5
26 gxh5

Euwe resigned on move 40.

Although the match was not yet half over, in effect it had already been decided. Euwe, unable to cope with Alekhine's crushing tactical blows, seemed dazed and dispirited. The final score was a lopsided 10–4 in Alekhine's favor, with eleven draws.

Euwe, ever the gentleman, acknowledged his opponent's superiority and blamed his personal catastrophe on physical and psychological factors. The latter, he said, had a particularly damaging effect in the second half of the match, when he was suffering from exhaustion.

Alekhine continued to play in tournaments (but no more matches) until World War II broke out, when virtually all international chess activity came to a halt. During the war a few tournaments were organized in Europe by the Nazis, but they were not significant despite the participation of Alekhine.

In 1946 Alekhine died. His body was found by a friend in a shabby hotel room in Portugal. He had been eating his supper, half of which remained on his plate. He was wearing a heavy greatcoat against the cold of his unheated room. On the table in front of him was a chess position he had been studying.

Alekhine's contributions to chess theory were extremely significant, especially in the openings. Many familiar variations in the King's Indian Defense, the Queen's Indian Defense, the Nimzo-Indian Defense, the Grünfeld Defense, the Reti Opening, and, of course, Alekhine's Defense, were very new in Alekhine's day, and he himself was in the forefront of the avant-garde.

Much of Alekhine's theoretical work in the openings sprang from his refusal to accept the prevalent notion that Black, because he moves second, must be satisfied to overcome White's natural initiative and achieve theoretical equality. Black, he felt, should have equal chances—equal *winning* chances—from the start. This conception of Black's role in the struggle is a keystone of modern opening theory—and of chess psychology as well.

Another of Alekhine's enduring contributions to chess was his method of preparation for important competitions. Fortunately for those who came after him, Alekhine wrote lengthy articles about Capablanca and Euwe, "psychoanalyzing" their styles, dissecting their openings, middlegames, and endgames.

Kotov and Yudovich, in *The Soviet School of Chess*, wrote:

Like Lasker, Alekhine considered a psychological approach necessary. Before each game in an important tournament, he said, the player should attentively study and weigh all the minuses in his opponent's play, and then prepare and force on him the position he least liked. Alekhine would face a theoretician with an unexpected and unknown variation. When playing a master who was weak on theory he would confound him with complex theoretical fine points.

Krogius, in his book on theoretical chess psychology, makes the point that Alekhine went beyond Lasker in psychological understanding: "He considered it necessary to account not only for the peculiarities of the play and character of his rivals, but also to anticipate their psychological preparation directed against him."

In the middlegame Alekhine had no equal. His combinations were particularly dangerous because, as many masters have pointed out, the point of a typical Alekhine combination came only at the end of a series of innocent-looking moves. He perfected the technique of misdirection, not only in his combinations but also in his overall strategies.

Alekhine, Russian by birth and training, left his homeland in 1922 for political reasons, and for a long time he was vilified in the Soviet press. But later he was reclaimed by the Soviets as one of the main pillars upon which the Soviet school of chess was founded.

■ ■ ■

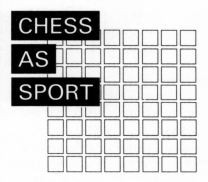

CHAPTER 3

CHESS
AS
SPORT

In 1946, while negotiating a match for the world championship with Mikhail Botvinnik of the Soviet Union, Alekhine suddenly died, leaving the title up for grabs. Urged by the Soviet Union and other countries to establish an orderly system of world championship competition, the International Chess Federation (FIDE) stepped in.

The first step was a match-tournament, held in 1948, among Botvinnik, Sammy Reshevsky, Paul Keres, Vasily Smyslov, and Max Euwe. This unique event was won decisively by Botvinnik, who thus became the first official FIDE world champion.

Alekhine's death and the emergence of FIDE brought to an end the era of the proprietary world championship. The champion's power to dictate match conditions favorable to himself had placed his challengers at a clear psychological disadvantage. He could even avoid an undesirable challenger by simply demanding an impossibly high purse or setting other difficult conditions. That's exactly how Alekhine managed to avoid a rematch with Capablanca (in the meantime playing two title matches with the much weaker Bogolyubov). And Lasker's longevity as champion certainly owed something to his canny use of the titleholder's power.

Soon after their revolution, the Soviets, capitalizing on the Russian people's historic love of chess and on the country's vast reserves of talented players, had instituted vigorous training programs in chess (as well as in other activities). Botvinnik's capture of the world title validated that policy and spurred the country to even greater efforts.

A year after winning the title, Botvinnik wrote that Soviet chess players were "bringing benefit to the Soviet state. . . . When we compete in international tournaments and defend the honor of our country, we recognize our duty before the Soviet people, before the Bolshevik party and the great cause of Lenin and Stalin."

Indeed, Soviet chess players sought success on the chessboard as though the very survival of their political system depended on it. In the Soviets' view, chess was not merely an art or a science or even a sport; it was what it had been invented to simulate: war.

This view of chess had a profound effect on the development of chess psychology, particularly through the work and achievements of the new world champion.

Mikhail Moiseevich Botvinnik was born in 1911 in St. Petersburg. He earned his master title in 1927 and became Soviet champion for the first time in 1931. By then he had also earned a university degree in electrical engineering, and in this field, too, he was to make valuable contributions.

The first of Botvinnik's three encounters with Alekhine, at Nottingham in 1936, was an interesting psychological battle. Both players were under great pressure. Alekhine, having lost the world title to Euwe in 1935, was trying to regain his confidence for the rematch scheduled for the following year. And, having left his homeland for political reasons, he must have been aware of the hostility of his opponent, a dedicated patriot. Botvinnik, appearing in only his second foreign tournament, needed to redeem himself after his disappointing tie for fifth at Hastings in 1935. And he needed to uphold his country's honor against this opponent in particular.

NOTTINGHAM 1936
Sicilian Defense

A. Alekhine	M. Botvinnik
1 e4	c5
2 Nf3	d6
3 d4	cxd4
4 Nxd4	Nf6
5 Nc3	g6
6 Be2	Bg7
7 Be3	Nc6
8 Nb3	Be6
9 f4	0-0
10 g4	

Alekhine, following his customary style, starts a dangerous, double-edged attack.

10 . . .	d5

Played in accordance with the well-known principle of responding to a flank attack with a reaction in the center. This temporary pawn sacrifice had been tried in the game Levenfish–Botvinnik a few months earlier at a tournament in Moscow, and after 11 e5 d4 12 Nxd4 Nxd4 13 Bxd4 Nxg4 Black was equal.

11 f5	Bc8
12 exd5	Nb4

"At first I could not understand why Alekhine was playing this opening," Botvinnik wrote later. "But when the position as shown arose, I guessed from his expression that he had something up his sleeve, was preparing some combination. I was right!"

13 d6!?

White's idea is to weaken Black's protection of the f6-square and then to exploit it: e.g., 13 . . . exd6 14 a3 followed by 15 g5 and 16 f6.

Keres later recommended 13 Bf3, a move that helped Fischer defeat Reshevsky in game two of their 1961 match.

13 . . .	Qxd6
14 Bc5	

44

An extremely unpleasant situation for Black. Botvinnik wrote: "At the critical point, in my search for escape I had to spend some twenty minutes in thought, and all that time Alekhine circled round and round our table. Summoning all my will power I managed to free myself from this strong 'psychological' pressure and find a way out of the trap."

14 ...	Qf4!
15 Rf1	Qxh2
16 Bxb4	Nxg4!

This second piece sacrifice saves the day. White has nothing better than to accept it and settle for a draw.

17 Bxg4	Qg3 +
18 Rf2	Qg1 +
19 Rf1	draw

In their second meeting, two years later in Amsterdam, Botvinnik was able to impose his own style of play on his opponent. Alekhine was now world champion again, having defeated Euwe in their return match in 1937.

AVRO 1938
Queen's Gambit Declined

M. Botvinnik	A. Alekhine
1 Nf3	d5
2 d4	Nf6
3 c4	e6
4 Nc3	c5
5 cxd5	Nxd5
6 e3	

When this game was played it was thought that Black could equalize easily after 6 e4 (as Euwe had recently done against Alekhine in the return match). The line has since been improved for White, and now it is not clear that Black can equalize at all.

6 . . .	Nc6
7 Bc4	cxd4
8 exd4	Be7
9 0-0	0-0
10 Re1	b6?

He should play 10 . . . Nxc3 and 11 . . . b6.

11 Nxd5!	exd5
12 Bb5	Bd7
13 Qa4	Nb8

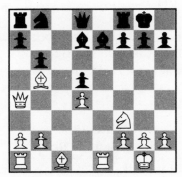

It is sad to see such a lover of active play as Alekhine forced to retreat so ignominiously. After 13 . . . Rc8, White can't win the a-pawn by 14 Bxc6 Bxc6 15 Qxa7 because of 15 . . . Bb4!, threatening both 16 . . . Bxe1 and 16 . . . Ra8. But the right answer to 13 . . . Rc8 is 14 Bd2, now really threatening to win the a-pawn.

14 Bf4	Bxb5
15 Qxb5	a6
16 Qa4	Bd6
17 Bxd6	Qxd6
18 Rac1	

White has both open files under his control, and Black has nothing to look forward to but a long, difficult defense without active play. Poor Alekhine! This was the kind of position he hated the most—which is why Botvinnik steered for it.

18 . . .	Ra7
19 Qc2	Re7
20 Rxe7	Qxe7
21 Qc7	Qxc7

Since White's queen cannot be permitted to establish itself in the heart of Black's position, this is forced. But the exchange gives Black no relief because White's remaining pieces are far more active.

22 Rxc7	f6
23 Kf1	Rf7
24 Rc8 +	Rf8
25 Rc3!	

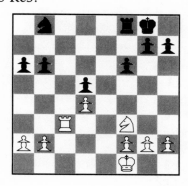

If Black could bring his king closer to the center, say to d6, he might hope for salvation; but the king is needed to protect the kingside pawns. Alekhine decides to advance those pawns so he can centralize his king, but he only creates new weaknesses.

25 . . .	g5
26 Ne1	h5

White's task is not as easy as it looks, for the slightest inaccuracy will let Black off the hook. An obvious plan for White is to get his knight to the center, but after 27 Nc2 Kf7 28 Ne3 Ke6, the knight is kept out of f5. If Black's h-pawn were on h6 instead of h5, then 29 g4 would allow the decisive occupation of f5 by White's knight. Alekhine avoided that danger with 26 . . . h5, but . . .

27 h4!

Now on 27 . . . Kf7 28 Nf3 g4 (*28 . . . Kg6 29 hxg5 fxg5 30 Ne5+*) 29 Ne1 Ke6 30 Nd3 and 31 Nf4, the knight finds a powerful post in the center.

27 . . .	Nd7
28 Rc7	Rf7
29 Nf3!	g4
30 Ne1	f5
31 Nd3	f4
32 f3	gxf3
33 gxf3	a5
34 a4	Kf8
35 Rc6	Ke7
36 Kf2	Rf5
37 b3	Kd8
38 Ke2	Nb8

A desperate attempt to free himself. If now 39 Rxb6 Kc7 followed by 40 . . . Nc6 with counterplay.

39 Rg6	Kc7
40 Ne5	Na6
41 Rg7+	Kc8
42 Nc6	

Now Black will lose material but without getting any counterplay. The concluding moves: 42 . . . Rf6 43 Ne7+ Kb8 44 Nxd5 Rd6 45 Rg5 Nb4 46 Nxb4 axb4 47 Rxh5 Rc6 (if *47 . . . Rxd4 48 Rf5* and White is ready to advance his h-pawn without hindrance) 48 Rb5 Kc7 49 Rxb4 Rh6 50 Rb5 Rxh4 51 Kd3 and Black resigned.

The advent of World War II put a stop to most international chess activity, but Botvinnik continued scoring impressive victories in Soviet events. When the war ended, he resumed his attempts to arrange a title match with Alekhine.

Alekhine at that stage of his life was a physical and psychological ruin, and his death spared him the agony of what would have been a humiliating defeat at Botvinnik's hands. There can hardly be any doubt about the result: Botvinnik dominated all of his great contemporaries even when they were at the top of their form: In the 1948 match-tournament, he defeated Smyslov 3–2, Keres 4–1, Reshevsky 3½–1½, and Euwe 3½–1½.

Botvinnik's forerunners in the psychological method, Lasker and Alekhine, were primarily tacticians; Botvinnik was a strategist of the highest order, as many of his games from the match-tournament showed. He was quite capable of accurate, imaginative tactics too, but he resorted to tactical complications only when he needed to get out of trouble or change the character of the game. The following game from the match-tournament is a perfect demonstration of how to create complications to exploit an opponent's time pressure.

MOSCOW–HAGUE 1948

S. Reshevsky

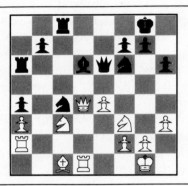

M. Botvinnik

White has been strategically outplayed. His pieces are tied up, and Black's threats, particularly . . . Ne5, are hard to meet. Botvinnik, realizing that further positional maneuvering would be futile, decides to take drastic action to change the course of the game. And now, with Reshevsky in time pressure, is the time to do it.

26 Nd5!?

This pawn sacrifice has two aims: first, to complicate the game in the hope that favorable tactical opportunities will turn up; second and more dangerous, to unsettle Reshevsky while he is in time pressure.

26 . . .	Nxe4
27 Re2	f5
28 g4(!)	

Shades of Alekhine! This is the point of White's twenty-sixth move. Reshevsky misses the correct reply 28 . . . Ng5!, after which all the complications would be in Black's favor; e.g., 29 Nxg5 Qxe2 30 Nf6+ gxf6 31 Qd5+ Kh8 32 Nf7+ Kh7 33 Qxf5+ (*33 Ng5+ fxg5 34 Qf7+ Kh8 35 Qf6+ Kg8 36 Qg6+ Kf8* and there is no perpetual check) 33 . . . Kg7 34 Bxh6+ Kxf7 and Black wins. After 29 Rxe6 Nxf3+ 30 Kg2 Nxd4 31 Rxd4 fxg4, Black has a sound extra pawn. The same is true of 29 Qd3 Nxf3+ 30 Qxf3 fxg4.

Reshevsky was certainly capable of calculating these variations, but not in time pressure. Botvinnik's decision to create complications when he did turns out perfectly.

| 28 . . . | Bc5(?) |

A typical time pressure move: Reshevsky attacks something to gain time.

| 29 gxf5 | Qxf5(?) |

Black could have emerged unscathed (though no longer with any advantage) after 29 . . . Bxd4 30 fxe6 Bxf2+ 31 Rxf2 Nxf2 32 Kxf2 Rxe6, with rook and two pawns for two pieces.

30 Qxe4	Qxh3
31 Nh2	Rf8
32 Nf4	forfeit

Black overstepped the time limit. Botvinnik's gamble had paid off.

For three years after winning the world title, Botvinnik played no competitive chess, devoting his attention instead to earning his doctorate in electrical engineering. But the new system set up by FIDE required the champion to defend his title every three years, so in 1951 he faced his first challenger, the first man to have survived FIDE's new series of elimination competitions: David Bronstein.

Like all the strong Soviet players who matured after the Revolution, Bronstein (born 1924) began his chess career at the Pioneers, a youth organization roughly comparable to our Boy Scouts but with much greater emphasis on the identification and development of career skills. Bronstein became a master at age sixteen, and in his first international tournament, Stockholm 1948, he was undefeated and took first place ahead of many established grandmasters.

Bronstein is a player of exceptional originality and creativity, especially in the middlegame. But he is bored by routine or simple positions, and his impatience has hurt him. I* vividly remember my first two games with him, played in the Moscow–Budapest team match in 1948–49. Both featured long endgames, in one of which I was a pawn down; yet both were drawn after about a hundred moves. Those games clearly showed Bronstein's dislike of simple endgames and the gaps in his endgame technique.

But Bronstein is a real fighter. Needing a win in the last round of the Budapest Interzonal in 1950 (one of FIDE's new elimination events), he surprised the great Keres with a risky pawn sacrifice and won the game, tying for first place. A year later, he and Boleslavsky

*This and all subsequent first-person pronouns refer to Pal Benko.

played a match to break the tie and decide which of them would challenge Botvinnik for the world championship. After the twelve scheduled games the score was tied, Bronstein again resorted to a surprise—this time an unsound move in the French Defense—and, as before, his surprised opponent lost the game.

Despite Botvinnik's six months of training for his title defense against Bronstein, he was often in trouble during the match and was behind in the score until the very end. There is no question that Bronstein had the more effective psychological strategy.

For example, although Bronstein was known to prefer 1 e4, he used that move only once in the match. As Black he resorted to the Dutch Defense, at that time a favorite of Botvinnik's, who was burdened with the psychological disadvantage of fighting against his own weapon. And Bronstein often was able to exploit Botvinnik's discomfort in unclear tactical situations by creating unexpected complications.

Botvinnik managed to tie the match at the last moment and keep his title (FIDE rules permitted the champion to remain champion until he was defeated) only through his belated discovery of Bronstein's Achilles' Heel—his impatience in simple positions, especially in the endgame. A careful study of the exceptionally rich games of this match shows that Botvinnik retained his crown largely by virtue of his superior endgame technique.

The English chess writer Robert Wade has written of Bronstein's "psychological genius which has on many occasions served him in good stead." There is no doubt that Bronstein's shrewd understanding of chess psychology was crucial to his success. Without it, his impetuous style and technical flaws might have relegated him to a minor career.

Three years after his narrow escape against Bronstein, Botvinnik faced a new challenger, Vasily Smyslov. Their first championship match, in 1954, ended in
a tie, and, again, this allowed Botvinnik to retain his
title. In 1957 Smyslov challenged again, this time successfully: With a decisive 12½–9½ win, he became the
new world champion.

FIDE's rules governing the championship entitled
a defeated champion to a rematch the following year.
Botvinnik, who had just turned forty-six and was expected to retire, surprisingly exercised that right.

Psychology played an important role in the 1958
rematch. Botvinnik resorted to an opening with which
he had not previously been identified, the Caro-Kann
Defense, and it helped him earn three victories in the
first three games. Smyslov never recovered. "Smyslov
lacked sufficient psychological stability," wrote Alexander Kotov. "Defeats had a demoralizing effect on
him."

Although Smyslov was one of the greatest players
of his time, perhaps the greatest of them all when he
was at his peak in the 1950s (he outscored Botvinnik
35–34 in their three matches, though he was champion for only one year), he was no chess psychologist.
If he had been, he, rather than Botvinnik, might have
been the dominant player of his generation.

Botvinnik used to describe himself modestly as *pri-
mus inter pares*, foremost among equals. But among
his rivals in the late 1950s, one player emerged—
erupted—who would have the most profound effect
on the game since Paul Morphy a century earlier.
Wherever chess was played or read about, the name
Mikhail Tal was on everybody's lips.

Tal was born in Latvia in 1936. He was only twenty-
one when, in 1957, he won the powerful Soviet championship for the first time. As if to prove that it was no

fluke, he won it again in 1958, and in the same year he won the Interzónal tournament in Portoroz. A year later, drawing energy from each new triumph, he outscored all the world's best players to win the Candidates' tournament and became, at twenty-three, the challenger for the world championship.

Tal's achievement at Portoroz was attributed by some to his "amazing good luck," considering the number of errors his opponents made. Sound familiar? Those are almost the exact words that had been used to describe Lasker's then incomprehensible successes. But as Reti realized after studying Lasker's games, it defies common sense to believe that a player can achieve such success on his opponents' errors: "The hypothesis of lasting luck," he wrote, "is too improbable."

Errors have nothing to do with luck; they are caused by time pressure, discomfort or unfamiliarity with a position, distractions, feelings of intimidation, nervous tension, overambition, excessive caution, and dozens of other psychological factors. The ability to create the psychological conditions in which the opponent is likely to make mistakes—that is Tal's special talent, which he possesses to a higher degree than any other player besides Bobby Fischer.

In my first encounter with Tal, at the Student Team Championship in Reykjavik 1957, I outplayed him early in the game but got into time pressure. Just then, at the worst possible moment for me, he sacrificed a piece. With too little time for calculation, I missed the winning reply. Then, still a piece ahead, I couldn't bring myself to take a draw but insisted on winning, and so I lost. Tal's piece sacrifice was unsound, as post-game analysis proved, but so what? It had served its purpose. Was this luck? Hardly. It was a perfect demonstration of practical chess psychology.

Although Tal has remained very near the pinnacle of world chess, the dashing style that made him one of the most popular chess players in history has been absent from his games for a long time. That style was based on a phenomenal tactical skill, an ability to calculate long and complicated variations accurately, a readiness, not to say eagerness, to take wild chances at the slightest provocation, and an uncanny instinct for introducing complications at the worst time for his opponent.

People called him a wizard, a magician, a sorcerer, "the devil from Riga," and similar terms, which only proved that they did not appreciate the real basis of his power. The "romantic" style, which was thought to have vanished around the time of Steinitz, had found a new champion in Tal, but it was a style that had been enriched by nearly a century of chess practice, and deepened and strengthened by the psychological insights of Lasker, Alekhine, and Botvinnik.

Tal was well aware of this. Discussing those three champions, he wrote:

> Through their efforts it has become accepted that there is . . . a subjective or perhaps psychological element in chess which one cannot and, indeed, should not attempt to escape. I believe most definitely that one must not only grapple with the problems on the board; one must also make every effort to combat the thoughts and will of the opponent.

All the elements of dramatic confrontation were present in the match in 1960 when World Champion Botvinnik faced his young challenger. On the one side Tal, the young tactician with a predilection for wildness; on the other Botvinnik, the mature strategist who relied on meticulous preparation. Youth versus age, art versus science.

And the match started with a surprise: Tal won the first game. Four draws followed, and in the sixth game Tal won again, this time with a spectacular piece sacrifice. Amazingly, the young Latvian was two points up on the world champion. Botvinnik, probably just as stunned as everyone else, committed a gross error in the very next game, and suddenly the score was 3–0 in Tal's favor. Although Botvinnik got a grip on himself and won the next two games, his opponent's adventurous style and youthful energy finally proved too much for him. The final score was a crushing 12½–8½. Tal, at twenty-four, was world champion.

After the match, some commentators tried to tarnish Tal's achievement by suggesting that the decisive factor was not his tactical brilliance but rather his psychological cunning. In his book on the match (one of the masterpieces of modern chess literature), Tal answered his critics with a terse, pragmatic defense of the psychological method: "I know I made what appeared to be bad moves at times, but they served the purpose of making my opponent use up time, figuring why I made such a move."

After losing the title, Botvinnik immediately began preparations to face Tal again in the rematch, scheduled for 1961. This time he was ready.

He had discovered that Tal, like most young attacking players, lacked a complete understanding of the endgame and would become impatient. So in the rematch Botvinnik followed a policy of exchanging queens early and relying on the most solid defensive systems to frustrate Tal's attacks. The result: after ten games Botvinnik led five wins to two, with three draws.

At that point Tal seemed to fall apart, losing three games in a row. That was too much. The final score

was ten wins to five, with six draws. Botvinnik for the
third time was crowned world champion.

Tal has been plagued by seriously bad health
throughout his life, and his frequent hospitalizations
and periods of severe pain have certainly limited the
successes his genius entitled him to. Although many
people blamed his health for the disaster in the second
match, it is also clear that Botvinnik rarely gave him
an opportunity to play the kinds of positions he liked.

The following game was played when Botvinnik
was leading six wins to three.

WORLD CHAMPIONSHIP, 1963
Game 13
King's Indian Defense

M. Botvinnik	M. Tal
1 d4	Nf6
2 c4	g6
3 Nc3	Bg7
4 e4	d6
5 f3	0-0
6 Be3	e5

After the match, Botvinnik wrote that his opponent
seemed to be in "an aggressive mood, as his choice of
opening shows. Taking note of this, White adopts the
correct decision—to exchange queens." Normally, if
White expects to create winning chances in this position, he keeps the queens on the board.

7 dxe5	dxe5
8 Qxd8	Rxd8
9 Nd5	Nxd5
10 cxd5	c6
11 Bc4	b5(?!)

Botvinnik's shrewd psychology already bears fruit. The best plan, according to theory, is 11 . . . cxd5 12 Bxd5 Nc6 with an even game. "Such a prosaic variation doesn't suite Tal," Botvinnik wrote, "and he plays for complications, in other words for compromising his own position."

12 Bb3	Bb7
13 0-0-0	c5

If the queens were still on the board, Black's queenside pawns might be something for White to worry about. But now this move serves only to give White a protected passed pawn.

14 Bc2

Preparing to break up Black's advancing pawns with a timely b3 and a4.

14 . . .	Nd7
15 Ne2	Bf8
16 Nc3	a6
17 b3	Rac8
18 Bd3	Nb6
19 Be2	Rd6
20 Kb2	f5

The attractive 20 . . . b4 21 Nb1 c4 22 bxc4 Nxc4+ 23 Bxc4 Rxc4 24 Rc1 would give White control of the c-file and bring Black closer to a lost endgame in view of White's passed pawn. So Black tries to open a second front on the kingside.

21 Rc1	Rf6
22 a4	bxa4

Further weakening his queenside and giving up control of key squares. But after 22 . . . b4 23 Nb1 the queenside would be blockaded and Black would have a weak c-pawn.

23 bxa4	a5
24 Kc2	c4
25 Rb1	Bb4
26 Na2	Bc5
27 Bxc5	Rxc5

28 Nc3

Botvinnik saw that 28 f4 would have won material by forcing Black's rook off the sixth rank, where it now protects the knight: if 28 . . . fxe4 29 fxe5, or 28 . . . exf4 29 e5. But "at this tense moment in the fifth hour of play," he wrote, "I did not want to present my opponent with even the slightest tactical counter-chances."

Botvinnik was criticized later for avoiding complications even at the risk of losing his advantage. Although post-game analysis confirmed the strength of

28 f4, Botvinnik has enough advantage to win any-way. The important factor from his point of view was to stick to his match strategy: denying Tal the kinds of positions he liked.

28 ...	Bc8
29 Rb2	Bd7
30 Rhb1	Bxa4 +
31 Nxa4	Nxa4
32 Rb8 +	

Black's extra pawn is meaningless, since his knight is out of play and White's rooks have broken through.

32 ...	Kg7
33 R1b7 +	Rf7
34 d6	Rxb7
35 Rxb7 +	Kf6
36 Rxh7	Rc8
37 d7	Rd8
38 Bxc4	Nc5
39 Rf7 +	Kg5
40 Bb5	fxe4
41 fxe4	Black resigned

There is no good defense to White's Re7-e8.

Botvinnik's next challenger, Tigran Petrosian, could not have been more different from Tal. Where-as Tal's style had elicited metaphors of the super-natural (wizard, magician, sorcerer, devil, etc.), Petrosian's seemed to evoke comparisons to the dan-gerously methodical predators of the animal world. Euwe wrote, "Petrosian is [like] a python who crushes his victim to death, or a crocodile ready to wait for hours for a suitable moment to strike the

■ ■ ■ ■ ■

decisive blow." Spassky later likened him to a porcupine who is most dangerous just when he appears to be caught.

Tal thrived on risk, Petrosian on avoiding risk. The cautious style that made Petrosian one of the hardest players in the world to defeat also gave him relatively few wins. In tournaments, Petrosian's lackluster style often produced unimpressive results and led to some criticism at home. In an article in the Russian press, he defended his style by claiming that it was necessitated by the nature of the game. "Obviously," he wrote, "many people forget that nowadays in chess, struggle for points prevails over creative considerations. . . . It is naive to think that it is expedient (let alone possible) for a player striving for the top place in a tournament to play every game all out, putting all his creative energy into every encounter."

Petrosian and Botvinnik played their match in 1963, when Botvinnik was fifty-two, Petrosian thirty-four. The age difference, which became a factor late in the match, was not Botvinnik's only handicap. When drawing up its rules for this match, FIDE had rescinded the provision entitling a defeated champion to a rematch within a year, a decision Botvinnik deeply resented.

Nevertheless, Botvinnik took an early lead by winning the first game and drawing the next three. With the champion's "draw odds" in his favor (under FIDE rules, if the score was tied after twenty-four games, the champion kept the title), his chances seemed excellent.

"After winning the first game," Petrosian wrote later, "Botvinnik apparently thought I would behave just like the other challengers. But I continued to play calmly, as if nothing had happened, so to speak."

Petrosian won game five, tying the score, and after another draw he won game seven. With a one-point lead to protect, Petrosian now turned on his draw-machine, and six draws followed. Botvinnik tried to sharpen the fight but was repeatedly frustrated, and as the match wore on it became obvious that his stamina was weakening. Although he managed to win another game, Petrosian won another three, and the match ended after twenty-two games with five wins for Petrosian, two for Botvinnik, and a final score of 12½–9½.

Botvinnik later wrote about Petrosian:

> He is not the most talented or the strongest player but certainly the most inconvenient player in the world! His ambition is not to play actively, but to paralyze his opponent's intentions. I personally did not succeed in adapting to his style, mainly because one is not able to change one's play easily at my age.

The most promising style to adopt against Petrosian, the former champion asserted, would be a combination of sound strategy and skillful tactics to create a great many very complicated positions in which Petrosian would be bound to lose his way. Only Boris Spassky managed to achieve this, in his second match with Petrosian.

After losing to Petrosian, Botvinnik retired from championship competition. He remained, however, one of the strongest tournament players in the world. I played against him three times. Our first two games were drawn, and at our third encounter, at Monte Carlo 1968, I was really looking for a win. Psychologically, it was quite an interesting fight.

MONTE CARLO 1968
English Opening

P. Benko	M. Botvinnik
1 c4	g6
2 g3	Bg7
3 Bg2	e5
4 Nc3	Ne7
5 e4	

Arriving in a roundabout way at the Closed Variation of the Sicilian Defense with colors reversed, a line
Botvinnik preferred when playing White.

5 . . .	d6
6 Nge2	Nbc6
7 d3	f5
8 Nd5	0-0
9 Be3	Be6
10 Qd2	Qd7
11 0-0	

Against Tal I probably would have played 11 h4,
starting an immediate attack on the kingside and
keeping the option of castling on the other wing.
Against a great defender like Botvinnik, however, I
chose to be prudent.

11 . . .	Rf7
12 Rae1	

Probably 12 Rac1 is better, with the idea of opening
a file on the queenside with an eventual b4 and c5.

12 . . .	Raf8
13 f4	

This is not necessary, since Black was not threatening to play . . . f4. Correct is 13 b4.

13 . . .   fxe4

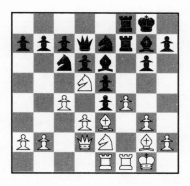

Analyzing the game later, Botvinnik wrote that Black's plan "is not without its positional novelty or psychological elements . . ." Black plans to trade off the light-squared bishops with . . . Bh3 to weaken White's kingside, and after the text move White's e-pawn will be weaker with White's bishop off the board.

14 dxe4   Nc8

Since Black is planning . . . Bh3, he needs the text move to keep his c-pawn protected. "Benko meets my idea," he wrote, "by an active and dangerous plan of counterplay on the queenside."

15 c5

I considered saving my bishop with 15 Rf2 (15 . . . Bh3 16 Bh1), but the text is more aggressive.

15 . . .	Bh3
16 b4	Bxg2
17 Kxg2	exf4
18 gxf4	Re8

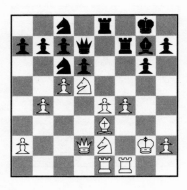

19 Ng3

"One can understand White's attempt to defend both his center pawn and his king position," Botvinnik wrote, "but in view of what now follows, 19 Nec3 is preferable. However, Benko is a player with an active style and doesn't like to retreat, so he chooses to play for a threatening-looking attack. By the way, this was the only game he lost at Monaco."

Psychologically, this is the turning point of the game. Of course I considered both possible knight moves, but finally I decided on the sharper one because I thought Botvinnik, seeing my attacking potential, would not dare provoke an assault. Underestimating my opponent was, of course, an error on my part, and Botvinnik's exploitation of it displays his own great psychological strength.

19 . . .   h5!

Now 20 . . . h4 is a very unpleasant threat, and 20 h4 Qg4 is no better. Although my confidence in White's attacking prospects was now somewhat cooler, I was committed to the attack and had to continue sharply.

          20 b5   N6e7
          21 f5!?   h4
          22 fxg6   Rxf1
          23 Rxf1

There's no turning back: 23 Nxf1 Qg4 + is easy for Black.

          23 . . .   hxg3
          24 Rf7

The threat is 25 Rxg7 + followed by 26 Qd4 +. Black finds the saving move.

          24 . . .   Be5!
          25 Bd4

The only way to continue the attack. If 25 Qe2 Qe6.

          25 . . .   Qg4

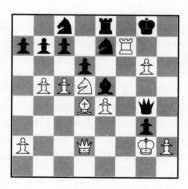

26 Rf4?

A mistake caused partly by time pressure and partly by my chagrin at the unexpected and unpleasant turn of events. I hoped for a draw after 26 . . . Bxf4 27 Nf6 + Kf8 28 Nh7 + and perpetual check, but Black doesn't cooperate.

I should have tried 26 Bxe5, but I didn't have time to calculate the long variations. Botvinnik claims a win after 26 Bxe5 gxh2 + 27 Bg3 Qxe4 + 28 Kxh2 Qxg6 (*28 . . . Qxd5 29 Qh6*) 29 Nxe7 + Rxe7 30 Rxe7 Nxe7 31 cxd6 Nf5! 32 Qd5 + Kf8 and "White could hardly hope for a draw." But that's a bit overoptimistic. B. Cafferty points out that White has 33 dxc7! Qxg3 + 34 Kh1. If then 34 . . . Nd6 35 Qxd6 + ; or if 34 . . . Ne7 35 Qd8 + Kf7 36 c8 (Q) Nxc8 37 Qxc8 Qe1 + followed by . . . Qe2 + and . . . Qxb5, Black wins a pawn, but his exposed king offers White good chances for perpetual check.

26 . . .   Qh5

Now it's all over. The conclusion was: 27 Bxe5 Qxh2 + 28 Kf3 Qxd2 29 Nf6 + Kg7 30 Nxe8 + Kxg6 31 Rf6 + Kh7 32 Bxg3 Qd3 + 33 Kf2 Qxb5 34 cxd6 Qxe8 and White resigned.

Several commentators graciously praised me for my courageous attack against the former world champion, but I had the feeling I was pushed into it.

Although Botvinnik is the only player to have lost the championship three times, he's also the only player to have *won* it three times. His exalted place in chess history is secure. All the leading Soviet players recognize his great contributions to chess in their country and the world.

Kotov wrote of Botvinnik that he "displayed a new

approach to chess as an art demanding deep scientific research. His studies and discoveries in opening theory, and his analysis of middlegames were a model of how chess strategy and tactics should be studied. His scientific training methods and competition regimen is worthy of emulation."

But it remained for Krogius to emphasize the psychological aspects of Botvinnik's game:

> Soviet players have studied and developed those methods of psychological preparation which were outlined by Lasker and Alekhine. Botvinnik was an important figure in this process—he developed his own system of preparation and training, which involved elements of great interest from the psychologist's point of view: (1) He drew up a personal, psychological characterization of the opponent; (2) he created maximum work capacity during play; and (3) he developed a certain psychological mood for each contest. Botvinnik conducted a well-informed, all-round psychological analysis of his opponent's play.

It would be a mistake, however, to give too much of the credit for the Soviets' considerable chess success to Botvinnik's methods. Much of the credit belongs to the Soviet chess movement as a whole. Players of talent are identified early and trained by professional teachers, many of them grandmasters. Their progress is carefully monitored, their successes appropriately rewarded. When a player has proved that he is ready to represent his country with honor, he is allowed to travel abroad to play in international tournaments. But he must not disappoint. We have seen more than one Soviet player achieve a poor or mediocre result in a foreign tournament and then disappear from the international arena.

The incredible longevity of Botvinnik's competitive

success undoubtedly owed a great deal to his Spartan self-discipline. Alekhine had gone into long periods of intense training before important matches, but Botvinnik adopted a severe training regimen as a permanent lifestyle. At various times he concentrated particularly on certain aspects of his training. For instance, to inure himself to typical tournament distractions, he would play training matches while a radio was blaring and his opponent was blowing smoke in his face. To avoid having to make even the most trivial daily decisions during an important event, he would always dress exactly the same way, eat and sleep at exactly the same times, travel to and from the playing site by exactly the same route, take his refreshment (always orange juice) at exactly the same time during each game.

One of the most remarkable aspects of Botvinnik's chess career is that he was able to perform so successfully for so long while pursuing a separate full-time career as an electrical engineer. We may never again see a top chess player with a dual career, for chess at the highest level has become too demanding to allow time or energy for anything else. Modern chess, like other serious sports and arts, is a way of life.

■■■

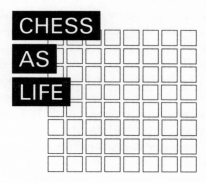

CHAPTER 4

CHESS AS LIFE

I first met Bobby Fischer when he was fifteen. The occasion was the Interzonal tournament at Portoroz, Yugoslavia, where Bobby became the youngest grandmaster in history. Since then we have met frequently at tournaments and on other occasions. We have analyzed chess games and positions together and have talked about chess and other subjects. I knew him very well—as well or better than anyone else in chess did. I have never observed at close range any other player as prodigiously gifted as he was.

At Portoroz, however, I was not quite ready to believe he was as good as some people said he was. He clearly had an important career in front of him, but at that moment he was still an unproven fifteen-year-old boy.

Players of that age have a low tolerance for positional pressure and often take unjustified risks to escape from even mildly unpleasant situations. Before

our game at Portoroz—my first against him—I decided
to try for a purely positional game in which he, playing
Black, would be under some slight pressure, at least at
first.

We met in the fourth round. In his first three games
Bobby had made two draws and had beaten Geza Füster, although he had escaped from a lost position in
that game. I wanted to get into the same opening variation but without tipping my hand: If I played the
opening the way Füster had, Bobby would smell a rat
and switch to another variation. I found a way to solve
that problem.

PORTOROZ 1958
King's Indian Defense

P. Benko	R. Fischer
1 d4	Nf6
2 c4	g6
3 Nc3	Bg7
4 e4	d6
5 f3	

Bobby played the King's Indian at every opportunity in those days. This move identifies the Sämisch
Variation, which Bobby eventually came to regard as
the strongest line against the King's Indian.

5 . . .	e5

This looks safe enough, since White gets no advantage by trading pawns and then queens. But it may be
premature, since Black might find it difficult to free
himself with . . . c5 later on.

6 Nge2	0-0
7 Bg5!	

Füster had played 7 Be3. The text move, with its unpleasant pressure on Black's knight, is more aggressive. Black can break the pin with 7 ... h6, of course, but after 8 Be3 White will win a tempo with Qd2, simultaneously attacking the h-pawn and clearing the first rank for queenside castling.

7 ...   exd4

Bothered by my bishop on g5, Bobby releases the central tension, which allows me to improve the position of my king knight. Bobby is trying to take advantage of the fact that my bishop is not on e3 protecting d4. It's not a bad idea, but maybe the execution could be improved; e.g., 7 ... Nc6 8 d5 Nd4 with an interesting pawn sacrifice: if 9 Nxd4 exd4 10 Qxd4 (*10 Nb5 c5 11 dxc6 bxc6 12 Nxd4 Qb6* with easy counterplay for Black) 10 ... h6 11 Bxf6 Bxf6, and Black's two good bishops would seem to give him enough play for the pawn, though the position is hard to judge.

8 Nxd4   Nc6
9 Nc2

The knight is headed for e3. Retreating it, even to its present modest square, is in line with the principle of avoiding piece exchanges when the opponent has a cramped position.

9 ...   Be6
10 Be2   h6
11 Bh4   g5(?)

Ah, the impetuousness of youth! Fischer is so eager to get rid of the unpleasant pin that he seriously weakens his kingside. The consequences of this move may not be immediately apparent, but it's the kind of move an experienced player would have avoided. In fairness to Fischer, however, he had an inferior position, and a good, active plan was hard to find.

12 Bf2	Ne5
13 Ne3	c6

Protecting d5 but weakening his d-pawn.

14 0-0	Qa5

Black is willing to give up his weak d-pawn, since after 15 Qxd6 Rfd8 16 Qa3 Qxa3 17 bxa3, White has an extra pawn but his queenside is in ruins. White's position is worth more.

Black's move is not just a simple trap; he is threatening ... Rfd8 followed by ... d5 to dispose of his weakness and get some activity for his pieces. It was becoming clear that although my young opponent had a few things to learn about this variation, he understood the game very well and was not to be trifled with.

15 Qd2!

Crossing Black up. I was also beginning to ogle his kingside weaknesses.

15 . . .   Rfd8
16 Rfd1   a6

Now Black will try for counterplay with . . . b5 instead of . . . d5.

17 a4   Qc7
18 a5

Expecting Black to prepare a break on the queenside, I had kept my rook on a1 so that I could play this move. White now has the possibility of an eventual Bb6.

18 . . .   c5

Black is thinking about counterplay with . . . Nc6, threatening both . . . Nd4 and . . . Nxa5. But to create that threat he abandons the d5-square, and this allows the immediate exploitation of the holes on his kingside.

Bobby had made it clear several times that he was ready to accept permanent positional weaknesses in return for active play. So far, however, his play has failed to materialize, and all he has are the weaknesses.

19 h4!

Threatening 20 hxg5, after which Ned5 would be extremely strong. Now Bobby must give up any idea of counterplay and concentrate instead on defending himself. He may not have paid much attention to this move, since White normally does not weaken the position of his own king.

19 . . .	Qe7
20 hxg5	hxg5
21 Nf5	Bxf5
22 exf5	g4

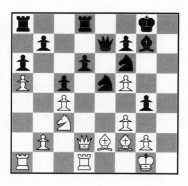

Black must make concessions. If 22 . . . Nh7 23 Nd5, or if 22 . . . Bh6 23 Be3. But now White's dark-squared bishop reestablishes that annoying pin.

23 Bh4	Qf8
24 fxg4	

Of course 24 Bxf6 wins a pawn, but then Black would be able to set up a blockade on the dark squares, counting on the opposite-color bishops to save him.

24 . . .	Nexg4
25 Bxg4	Nxg4
26 Qg5	

76

Much stronger than taking the exchange, which would give Black a chance for counterplay after . . . Bd4 + .

26 . . .	Nf6
27 Rd3	

Threatening Rg3. If 27 . . . Kh8 (or . . . *Kh7*) 28 Qxf6! wins.

27 . . .	Nh7
28 Qg4	f6

There is no other way to stop White from playing f6. Even in my usual time pressure I had no trouble finding good moves in this position, since Black hasn't even a whisper of counterplay.

29 Nd5	Qf7
30 Re1	Re8
31 Rde3	Re5
32 Bg3	Rxe3
33 Rxe3	Re8
34 Re6	Ng5
35 Rxd6	Re4
36 Rd8 +	Kh7
37 Bf4	Bh6

Hastening the end, but Qh4 + would have won soon anyway.

38 Rd7	Re1 +
39 Kf2	

Going to h2 is even simpler, insisting on winning the queen. Here, one move before the time control, the clock was a factor.

39 . . .	Ne4+
40 Kxe1	Qxd7
41 Qg6+	Black resigned

Fischer lost this game because of his impatience. Finding himself on unfamiliar ground (a natural consequence of his inexperience) and in a passive, slightly inferior position, he created serious weaknesses in his eagerness for active play. It was a position that required long, patient defense. Most players, especially young ones, dislike defending positions like that, but sometimes there's no alternative.

Bobby learned from that game, as he did from every loss. The next time we played, two years later, I again tried something new against his inevitable King's Indian Defense, but this time he handled the opening much better. Bobby was still a teenager, however, and still made mental errors typical of teenagers. Though he safely negotiated the opening, his overconfidence blinded him to danger.

BUENOS AIRES 1960
King's Indian Defense

P. Benko	R. Fischer
1 d4	Nf6
2 c4	g6
3 g3	Bg7
4 Bg2	0-0
5 Nc3	d6
6 Nf3	Nc6
7 h3?!	

The usual choices at the time were 7 0-0 and 7 d5. By now Bobby was a real expert on this opening, so, as in our previous game, I wanted to get him out of the books and into unfamiliar territory.

The idea of this move is simply to prepare Be3 without having to worry about . . . Ng4, but it clearly loses a tempo. My opinion at the time was that the strategic objective was worth a tempo, but I also had a psychological trap in mind. Grandmaster Edmar Mednis wrote of this move that it was "based strictly on psychological factors"; i.e., on White's hope that Black would "overreach himself in storming a safe bastion." Contrary to my hopes, however, Fischer achieves a good position and turns my experiment into a failure. But he then falls victim to another kind of psychological pitfall.

7 . . .	e5
8 0-0	

Maybe 8 Be3 should be played right away, but I was worried about 8 . . . Re8 9 0-0 exd4 10 Nxd4 Rxe3. White could avoid that with 9 dxe5, but it's too drawish (I was looking for winning chances), or with 9 d5, after which Black's rook would be misplaced on e8— as would White's bishop on e3.

8 . . .	exd4
9 Nxd4	Nxd4
10 Qxd4	Be6!

Developing rapidly to harass White's exposed queen. If 11 Bxb7 Bxh3, proving the disadvantage of the move h3.

11 Qh4

Seems best. 11 Qd3 Nd7 looks strong for Black.

11 . . .	Nd7!

Although it looks simple, a maneuver like this is not easy to find. Black now threatens to gain the upper hand by trading off White's active queen.

| 12 Bg5 | f6 |
| 13 Be3 | |

Unfortunately, 13 Bh6 loses the c-pawn after 13 . . . g5.

| 13 . . . | g5!? |

Later I saw this move mentioned somewhere. Though it had been given a question mark, nothing better was suggested. It's not a bad move, for the alternatives allow White to consolidate. Now White's queen gets pushed around some more, giving me real misgivings about my opening idea.

14 Qd4

If 14 Qe4 Re8 with continuing discomfort for White's queen.

14 . . .	f5
15 Qd2	f4!
16 gxf4	gxf4
17 Bxf4	

The pawn must be accepted. If 17 Bd4 Ne5 threatening . . . Qh4 with a strong attack.

| 17 . . . | Nb6 |

The point of Bobby's pawn sacrifice. He threatens to activate his knight with . . . Nxc4, and the c-pawn can't be protected by 18 b3 because of 18 . . . Rxf4.

18 Qe3

Trying to make things as difficult as possible for Black, and hoping to turn my dubious seventh move into a mere lost tempo that gave Black equal chances.

18 . . .   Qf6

This may be where Black begins to go wrong. Though the queen seems to be in an aggressive position at the moment, it will prove to be misplaced on the kingside. The quieter 18 . . . Qd7 looks better, keeping the initiative.

19 Bg5   Qg6
20 Qg3

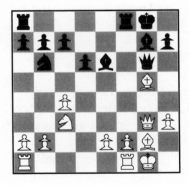

20 . . .   Nxc4

Thanks to White's sly queen move, this capture does not gain a tempo (the knight would now be attacking the queen had it remained on e3), which gives White time to take action. Either 20 . . . h6 or 20 . . . Rae8 would have been better.

Fischer's error was the result of overconfidence. He knew he was getting the advantage and probably thought there was no danger. He even seemed to have expected my reply, though obviously he misjudged its strength.

21 Nd5!

This disagreeable move threatens both Ne7 + and Nxc7, and 21 . . . Bxd5 simply loses a piece after 22 Bxd5 + .

21 . . .   Qf7

Bobby played this rather quickly, defending the c-pawn and the e7-square and threatening . . . Bxd5. But his best chance was 21 . . . Rf7, giving up the exchange (22 Ne7 +) but getting the b-pawn as compensation.

22 Bh6

Very strong. Black still can't play 22 . . . Bxd5, and the threat is 23 Bxg7 followed by 24 Nxc7. Now Black loses the exchange without getting a pawn for it.

22 . . .	c6
23 Bxg7	Qxg7
24 Qxg7 +	Kxg7
25 Nc7	Kf6
26 Nxa8	Rxa8
27 b3	Black resigned

Bobby's resignation came as a surprise, since 27 . . . Na3 would have offered strong resistance, though White's win was fairly certain. (I was even more surprised ten years later when he told me he had resigned this game prematurely! Even after all that time, he still looked at his old games, especially the ones he lost.) I think he gave up early because he simply found it distasteful to play positions in which he had no chance to be active.

I am not proud of that game: My opening novelty was a strategic failure, and I won only because of Bobby's overconfidence later on.

The basis of my psychological trap was Fischer's well-known love for the initiative, which is essentially an advantage in time. He believed—as have other players and theoreticians—that White's first-move advantage, properly exploited, should amount to virtually a forced win. (This idea may not be as exaggerated as it seems. Of the nineteen games I played against Fischer, I lost only one with White, missing a forced win, and seven with Black.) Svetozar Gligoric, writing in *How to Open a Chess Game* (R.H.M. Press, 1973), observed that Fischer's "secret weapon" was his extraordinary understanding of time in chess and his genius for exploiting a loss of time by his opponent.

In an interview, Fischer was once asked whether he used psychology against his opponents. "I don't believe in psychology," he replied. "I believe in good moves." That sounds very much like the remark of Fischer's great hero, Steinitz, cited in the first chapter ("So far as I am concerned my opponent might as well be an abstraction or an automaton"), but it was just posturing on Fischer's part. Although his contributions to practical chess psychology were not as significant as Lasker's, Alekhine's, or Botvinnik's, he was well aware of his predecessors' psychological methods and used them effectively.

What was most important to Fischer psychologically was his own sense of well-being. Before and during his match with World Champion Boris Spassky in Reykjavik 1972, the endless bitter arguments about what seemed to be trivia—the locations of the television cameras, the height of the chairs, the lighting above the chessboard, the size of the chess pieces, the dimensions of the squares they moved on—seemed almost comical to many of us at the time. But they were not trivial or comical to Fischer.

For Fischer, chess was life. He had overcome incredible obstacles to get where he was at that moment, to become the challenger for the world championship. This match was the goal of his entire life, his sole mission on earth, and the conditions in which the struggle would be waged had to be perfect in every detail. He was sure he was the greatest chess player in history, and he was about to prove it for the whole world to see. Nothing could be left to chance or to another's choosing. Everything had to be brought into harmony so that perfection could be achieved.

For a long time it seemed that the match would never start. Fischer's demands caused one postponement after another, and the Russians and the Icelandic organizers both came close to throwing up their hands in exasperation more than once.

Fischer was reported to have said that he deliberately delayed the start of the match to "psych out" Spassky. But that remark was merely a sop to satisfy the press. How else could he have explained his extraordinary behavior to people incapable of understanding him? The truth, even if he could have found the words to express it, would have been taken only as further evidence of his eccentricity.

The truth was that Fischer was quite ready to sacrifice the entire match if even the slightest detail did not meet his standards. But that doesn't mean he ig-

nored his adversary. Years earlier, Fischer had stated
publicly that Soviet chess politicians unfairly influ-
enced the results of international tournaments by having their players prearrange draws with one another.
Though he liked and respected Spassky personally,
Fischer considered him, as a Russian, an instrument
of Soviet policy. Fischer's guiding philosophy was,
therefore, "whatever is good for Spassky is bad for
me." There was no need to analyze Spassky's wishes
objectively to decide whether to oppose them or not;
they were opposed *a priori*, because they were
Spassky's.

Spassky may indeed have been psyched out, but
only partly because of Fischer's behavior. Spassky was
being pulled in several different directions at once. He
liked and admired Fischer, but it was his job to uphold his country's honor on the world stage. At the
same time, he had to be true to his own sense of honor.
At one point, after one of Fischer's delays, Spassky's
superiors in Moscow ordered him to come home and
claim the match by default. Spassky, at considerable
risk, refused. The match must be played, he said, because it would be good for chess and because a title
won by default would have little value.

The uncertainty about the match combined with
the pressure from Moscow must have had a profound
psychological effect on him. And his empathy with
Fischer could not have made things any easier.
Spassky believed strongly in the justice of Fischer's
lifelong fight for more respect and better playing conditions for grandmasters, and he openly admired Fischer's games—not a wise position for a Soviet
grandmaster to take in those days. One European
grandmaster close to both players during the match
suggested afterward that although Spassky had
played better overall, he had subconsciously wanted

to lose because he shared Fischer's sense of mission and felt he could not deny him his destiny.

Fischer's preparation for the match was concerned mainly with the choice of openings, but there were other psychological considerations too. I spoke with Bobby many times by phone while he was in training at Grossinger's resort hotel in upstate New York. I repeatedly stressed three points:

1. Although Bobby had never beaten Spassky, he would do it this time.
2. Bobby should use openings he had never played before, and should switch openings often to confound Spassky's well-known ability in match play to adjust quickly to the style of his opponent. Also, the use of new openings would cross up Spassky's opening preparations.
3. He would have to avoid the overconfidence that had cost him points in the past. He should not try too hard to win when victories were not needed. If he had a two- or three-point advantage in the match score, he should sit back and play it safe, placing the burden of having to win on Spassky.

All these factors, as the match itself shows, were crucial to Fischer's eventual victory.

Bobby's greatest psychological achievement of the match came in the third game, his first win ever against Spassky. He had thrown away the first game by blundering in a dead-drawn position and had forfeited the second game without play. With the score 2–0 in Spassky's favor, and considering the champion's draw odds (the FIDE rule that the champion would retain the title in case of a tied match was still in effect), Fischer's chances looked bleak. Most observers felt that the match was already effectively over and that Bobby would not continue with such a handicap. It is still hard for me to understand how he found the strength and courage to continue the match under those conditions.

Spassky himself must have felt that his opponent faced a hopeless task, and maybe it was his sympathy for Bobby that led him to agree to play the third game in a small room backstage, out of sight of the spectators. Bobby had been engaged in a running feud with various officials and entrepreneurs over the use of television cameras, and had threatened to forfeit the entire match, which would have been financially disastrous for the match's sponsors. The use of the backstage room was intended as a temporary compromise to allow the match to continue while the controversy was being resolved. But it had a costly psychological effect on Spassky.

WORLD CHAMPIONSHIP, 1972
Game 3

R. Fischer

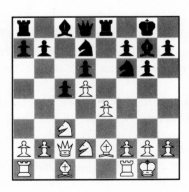

B. Spassky

11 . . .   Nh5!

This must have come as a shock to Spassky, a classical player. Though it violates classical opening principles—not to move an already developed piece before developing the other pieces, not to put a knight at the edge of the board, not to allow your pawns to become doubled and isolated—its main idea is a dynamic one: it forces the opening of lines against the enemy king and helps the development of Black's queen and queen bishop.

12 Bxh5

In view of Black's threat simply to plant his knight on f4, White has very little choice. If 12 g3 Ne5, or 12 f4 Bd4+ 13 Kh1 Ndf6, and in either case all of Black's pieces come charging into action against a weakened White kingside.

12 . . .   gxh5
13 Nc4

This obvious move gives Fischer no trouble. Smyslov suggested 13 Ne2; in a game between Gligoric and Kavalek right after this match (Skopje 1972), after 13 a4 Ne5 14 Nd1! Qh4 15 Ne3 Ng4 16 Nxg4 hxg4 17 Nc4 Gligoric's knight on c4 was more active than Spassky's in this game.

But it takes time to discover such possibilities. Spassky was facing this position for the first time.

13 . . .   Ne5
14 Ne3   Qh4
15 Bd2   Ng4

Now White is forced to straighten out Black's pawns.

16 Nxg4	hxg4
17 Bf4	Qf6
18 g3?	

Weakening the light squares on the kingside as well as the e-pawn, which White will now be unable to protect with f3. Since White eventually loses that pawn, this move may be considered the decisive mistake. Spassky had to play 18 Bg3, but he must have been worried about 18 . . . h5 threatening . . . h4. In that case, though, White gets counterchances with 19 Nb5. White could also have played 18 Bd2, intending to start action on the kingside with f3 or f4.

18 . . .	Bd7
19 a4	b6

Preparing . . . a6 and then . . . b5 (but not *19 . . . a6? 20 a5*).

20 Rfe1	a6
21 Re2	b5
22 Rae1	

If 22 axb5 axb5 23 Rxa8 Rxa8 24 e5 Ra1+ 25 Kg2 dxe5, White's king is dangerously exposed.

22 . . .	Qg6
23 b3	Re7
24 Qd3	Rb8
25 axb5	axb5
26 b4	c4

| 27 Qd2 | Rbe8 |
| 28 Re3 | h5 |

Black has plenty of time to improve his position before winning the e-pawn.

| 29 R3e2 | Kh7 |
| 30 Re3 | Kg8 |

Bobby must have been enjoying this: He had never had Spassky on the ropes before and was making him sweat. White was also in mild time pressure.

31 R3e2	Bxc3
32 Qxc3	Rxe4
33 Rxe4	Rxe4
34 Rxe4	Qxe4
35 Bh6	

White's only chance is an endgame with opposite-color bishops.

35 . . .	Qg6
36 Bc1	Qb1
37 Kf1	

Trying to get his king out of its cage. If White can bring his king to the queenside, maybe he can use it to blockade Black's passed pawn.

37 . . .	Bf5
38 Ke2	Qe4+
39 Qe3	Qc2+
40 Qd2	Qb3

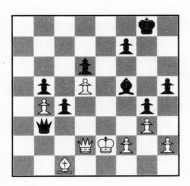

41 Qd4

In an interview after the match, Spassky said he had been so upset at this point in the game that he moved too quickly, making the mistake of allowing Fischer to be the one to seal his move before adjournment. He should have sealed here himself, he said, and the move should have been 41 Ke1, "with a chance to salvage the draw."

One suggested variation is 41 . . . Qf3 42 Qg5 + Bg6 43 Qe3 Qh1 + 44 Kd2 Qxd5 + 45 Kc3, but if that's the best White can do, Spassky's hope for a draw was too optimistic. Black should win with two extra pawns, especially since White's king is exposed and unable to blockade effectively with queens on the board.

41 . . .   Bd3 +

The sealed move. White has no hope: if 42 Ke3 Qd1 43 Bb2 Qf3 +, or 43 Qb2 Qf3 + 44 Kd4 Qe4 + 45 Kc3 Qe1 + and mates. When Spassky showed up to play the adjournment and saw the sealed move, he resigned at once.

"My acceding to Fischer's groundless demand to play in a closed room was a big psychological mistake," Spassky said after the match. The rest of the games were played in the main auditorium.

In game four, Spassky, as Black, came close to winning against Fischer's favorite Sicilian variation, thanks to well-prepared analysis by the Soviet team. Bobby won game five, tying the score, and in game six, with the White pieces, he wisely decided to switch openings. For the first time in his adult life, Fischer was on the White side of the Queen's Gambit.

WORLD CHAMPIONSHIP, 1972
Game 6
Queen's Gambit Declined

R. Fischer	B. Spassky
1 c4	e6
2 Nf3	d5
3 d4	Nf6
4 Nc3	Be7
5 Bg5	0-0
6 e3	h6
7 Bh4	b6

The Tartakower Variation, a long-time Spassky favorite. Fischer, knowing ahead of time that he would play queenside openings, must have been prepared for this variation, but Spassky, not expecting Fischer to play a queenside opening, probably did little, if any, special pre-match analysis of this opening.

Spassky had to base his preparations on the expectation that Fischer would continue to play 1 e4, since he had no way of predicting what Bobby might play

instead. As a matter of fact, Fischer might never have
switched from 1 e4 if his games with White had been
going well. But game four showed that Spassky was
ready to meet Bobby's kingside openings.

8 cxd5	Nxd5
9 Bxe7	Qxe7
10 Nxd5	exd5
11 Rc1	Be6

The regular move, since the bishop stands better
here than on the long diagonal. The purpose of . . . b6
was not to prepare . . . Bb7 but to support an eventual
. . . c5.

12 Qa4	c5
13 Qa3	Rc8
14 Bb5!	

A Russian invention. The idea is to exchange the
bishop for Black's knight when it goes to d7 to support
the c-pawn.

14 . . .	a6

Is this weakening necessary? Black can break the
pin with 14 . . . Qb7 and not worry about his c-pawn,
since if White takes the time to win it, he will fall
seriously behind in development.

15 dxc5	bxc5
16 0-0	Ra7

This was the move Yefim Geller played against the
inventor of White's maneuver, Semyon Furman, the
chief trainer of Anatoly Karpov. Geller got into trou-

ble and later recommended 16 . . . Qb7, but the situation is not clear after 17 Ba4.

17 Be2   Nd7
18 Nd4

A strong move. It is generally a good strategy to exchange minor pieces when working against the "hanging pawns" on c5 and d5. Fischer used to say that trading a knight for a bishop was "winning the minor exchange," a maxim that originated with Steinitz, one of Fischer's heros.

18 . . .   Qf8
19 Nxe6   fxe6
20 e4!

Breaking up the black center and opening lines for the queen and bishop.

20 . . .   d4

This advance does wonders for White's bishop. Spassky had three better moves: 20 . . . dxe4, 20 . . . c4, and 20 . . . Nf6.

21 f4

With the black center immobilized, White can use his kingside majority to break through.

21 . . .   Qe7
22 e5   Rb8
23 Bc4   Kh8
24 Qh3   Nf8

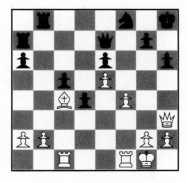

After 24 . . . Rxb2 25 Bxe6 White's kingside pawns would be much more dangerous than Black's queenside pawns. After 24 . . . Re8 and 25 . . . Nb6 White has Bd3 and Qh5, aiming for Qg6. The text move is passive, but Spassky had used up too much time in the early stages to begin looking for counterplay now. All he can do is to try to keep his position from falling apart.

25 b3	a5
26 f5	

Unconcerned that this move ruins his pawn position, Bobby goes for direct attack.

26 . . .	exf5
27 Rxf5	Nh7
28 Rcf1	Qd8
29 Qg3	Re7
30 h4	Rbb7
31 e6!	

Very strong. Fischer invites his opponent's knight to f6, where he would immediately snap it off with Rxf6.

31 . . .	Rbc7
32 Qe5	Qe8
33 a4	

Black can do nothing while White calmly plugs up possible avenues of counterplay.

33 . . .	Qd8
34 R1f2	Qe8
35 R2f3	Qd8
36 Bd3	

The threat is Qe4, and there is nothing that Black can do about it.

| 36 . . . | Qe8 |
| 37 Qe4 | Nf6 |

If 37 . . . Rxe6 38 Rf8+ followed by mate.

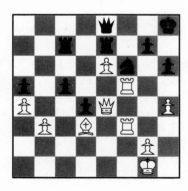

| 38 Rxf6! | gxf6 |
| 39 Rxf6 | |

There is no defense. An active try like 39 . . . Qh5 would be met by 40 Rf8+ Kg7 41 Qh7+ and mate.

39 . . .	Kg8
40 Bc4	Kh8
41 Qf4	Black resigned

If 41 . . . Rc8 42 Rxh6 + Kg8 43 Qg4 + Rg7 44 e7 + .

Ivo Nei, one of Spassky's seconds in Reykjavik, wrote that this game had "without doubt a psychological influence—Fischer showed that he was also very much at home in closed openings . . ."

Fischer went on to win the match and became world champion. As the time approached for him to defend his title in 1975, he became embroiled in a dispute with FIDE over various match rules. Some of Fischer's demands were considered by many experts to be unfair, while other experts, citing historical precedent and proving that Fischer's theories were logical and sound, came to his defense.

FIDE, under powerful pressure from the Soviets and their political allies, finally rejected a key Fischer demand, and he resigned his title. He soon dropped out of sight. The greater part of his life had been devoted to his quest for the world championship; having attained it, his life's work was over.

■■■

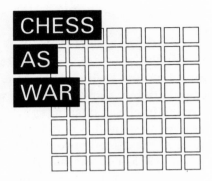

CHAPTER 5

CHESS
AS
WAR

When Fischer discarded the world championship crown, it landed on the head of the man who had been waiting in the wings to play him for it, Anatoly Karpov. Although he received the title without having actually won it, Karpov subsequently proved convincingly that he was worthy of being called world champion. He won most of the tournaments in which he participated, and he successfully defended his title in two epic matches against a most determined challenger, Viktor Korchnoi.

Karpov is a technician, more interested in efficiency than in artistry. Such a player, needless to say, is no psychologist. Nevertheless, his matches with Korchnoi, particularly the first title defense in 1978, held in Baguio City, the Philippines, were struggles in which the psychological battles pushed chess into the background.

Korchnoi had lost the final Candidates' match to Karpov in 1974, placing the latter in position to receive the title when Fischer abdicated the following year. Even before that match, however, their personal animosity had been growing. When Korchnoi defected from the Soviet Union in 1976, his festering contempt for the Soviet political system, and for Karpov particularly—who proudly represented that system—blossomed into overt hostility. When the title match began in 1978, Korchnoi intended not only to destroy his opponent but also to discredit the entire Soviet political apparatus with a single stroke.

The match was a field day for journalists. The two players refused to shake hands and openly insulted each other in statements to the press. Korchnoi, who at the time was officially a citizen of no country, insisted on displaying the Swiss flag on the chess table alongside Karpov's hammer and sickle. The Russians objected, wanting the hated defector to display no flag at all.

A member of Karpov's entourage, Dr. Vladimir Zukhar, a psychologist from Moscow's School of Medicine, sat in the second row during every game and stared intently at Korchnoi. Supporters of Korchnoi, suspecting that Zukhar was trying to exercise some sort of mind control, attempted to break Zukhar's concentration by sitting nearby and staring intently at *him*. Korchnoi eventually complained to the match referee, and Zukhar was banished to the rear of the auditorium.

In mid-match, two members of an obscure religious cult, convicted terrorists out on bail, arrived to offer Korchnoi their support, or perhaps to counteract Dr. Zukhar's influence. Their presence infuriated the Russians, who managed to have them banished not only from the auditorium, where they had sat staring at Karpov, but also from Korchnoi's rented villa and ultimately from Baguio City.

Korchnoi donned dark glasses during play. Karpov started swiveling back and forth in his chair. When Korchnoi complained about the swiveling, Karpov said he would stop if Korchnoi took off his glasses.

On and on went the war of nerves while, on the chessboard, the match swung first in Karpov's favor, and then, incredibly, was tied after game 31. But Korchnoi lost game 32, which ended the match—or did it? Since during that game Dr. Zukhar had been once again seen in the fourth row giving Korchnoi the evil eye, Korchnoi refused to continue after adjournment and protested the game. But to no avail. The match was over, and Karpov was still world champion.

Three years later, the two men played again, and again Karpov won, though this time the off-board shenanigans were not nearly as much fun. Korchnoi was then fifty-four years old, and after losing that match he was finally forced to admit that he could not fight both Karpov and the relentlessly advancing years.

Karpov's two title defenses thus far had been against a man twenty years his senior. In 1984 he came up against a dangerous new talent ten years his junior: Gary Kasparov, who had become the challenger by demolishing three powerful opponents— Belyavsky, Korchnoi, and Smyslov—in a two-year series of candidates' matches.

Karpov and Kasparov are completely unalike, both on and off the board. In life, Karpov is aloof and taciturn, Kasparov gregarious and outspoken. In politics, Karpov is a willing representative of the old-line communist system, Kasparov an eager adherent of glasnost. In chess, Karpov is a technician, Kasparov a creator.

Before their first match for the title, Kasparov admitted that his rival was stronger in certain types of positions and had the better endgame technique, but where imagination was called for, Kasparov claimed superiority. This was an admirably realistic assessment. Kasparov's problem, though, was that Karpov didn't let him get the kinds of positions in which he could use his superior gifts. In game after game, Kasparov fell victim to Karpov's superb endgame technique, losing four of the first nine games while winning none. The match already seemed hopeless.

At this point, Kasparov gave up trying to crush his opponent and began to play for draws, reportedly following Botvinnik's advice to try to tire out his older rival. There ensued an incredible string of seventeen consecutive draws. Karpov then won again (game 27) and needed but one more win to end the match. But as in the 1978 Korchnoi match, he seemed unable to deliver the final blow.

Kasparov finally scored his first win in game 32, and after another series of fourteen draws, he won again in game 47. That game is a good indication of the toll the match had taken on Karpov.

WORLD CHAMPIONSHIP, 1985
Game 47
Queen's Gambit Declined

A. Karpov	G. Kasparov
1 Nf3	Nf6
2 c4	e6
3 d4	d5
4 Nc3	c6
5 Bg5	Nbd7
6 e3	Qa5

The Cambridge Springs Variation—and the first surprise. Though Kasparov had played White against this line, most recently in his Candidates' match with Smyslov, he had never ventured it with Black. It was therefore probably not in Karpov's "computer."

7 cxd5	Nxd5
8 Qd2	N7b6

Surprise number two. Smyslov had chosen 8 . . . Bb4 twice in the above-mentioned match, losing both times. Karpov, obviously unprepared to meet this line, took thirty-six minutes to find a reply, and he came up with a timid simplifying exchange instead of the fighting 9 Bd3.

9 Nxd5	Qxd2 +
10 Nxd2	exd5

The game looks drawish after 10 . . . cxd5, but this recapture keeps the position unbalanced. Black has already equalized.

11 Bd3	a5
12 a4!?	

Another timid move, weakening the b4-square and thereby giving up any possibility of queenside play.

12 . . .	Bb4
13 Ke2	Bg4 +
14 f3	Bh5
15 h4	0-0
16 g4	Bg6
17 b3	Bxd3 +
18 Kxd3	Rfe8
19 Rac1	

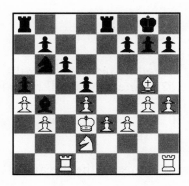

White is obviously worried that Black will play . . . c5. Therefore:

    19 . . .   c5

Suddenly Black becomes aggressive. If 20 dxc5 Nd7 21 c6 Ne5+ and the knight comes to life.

    20 Bf4   Rac8
    21 dxc5   Nd7
    22 c6

The prudent course was to simplify with 22 Bd6, but Black would still have the edge after 22 . . . b6 23 c6 Nc5+ 24 Bxc5 bxc5.

    22 . . .   bxc6
    23 Rhd1   Nc5+
    24 Kc2   f6
    25 Nf1

White can't find an active plan, and meanwhile Black strengthens his position.

    25 . . .   Ne6
    26 Bg3   Red8
    27 Bf2   c5

28 Nd2	c4!
29 bxc4	Nc5
30 e4?	

Stronger resistance was possible with 30 Ra1, but after 30 . . . Nd7 White would still be in trouble.

| 30 . . . | d4 |
| 31 Nb1 | |

There was no defense to the threat of 31 . . . d3+ 32 Kb2 Bxd2 33 Rxd2 Rb8+ and 34 . . . Nb3.

31 . . .	d3+
32 Kb2	d2
White resigned	

Karpov's usual toughness was not to be seen in that game, and the exhausted champion lost the next game too.

At that point, after forty-eight games and months of bitter struggle, the match was broken off by FIDE President Florencio Campomanes. To continue, he said, would be to risk the health of the players.

But Kasparov wanted to go on, although he was behind in the score. Most chess people thought, as did Kasparov, that Karpov was behind Campomanes's decision. Karpov had lost twenty pounds since the match started and had obviously reached the limits of his physical and mental endurance. This was a six-win match with no limit on the number of games, and Karpov had stood with five wins for the last twenty-one games, unable to score that one final win to end the torture.

After six months of recuperation, a new match began in Moscow. Technically, it was not a rematch but a restart of the original match, which had not ended naturally.

The players were not on good terms, to put it mildly; this, like the 1978 Karpov–Korchnoi encounter, was a grudge match. Each player did what he could to upset the other. Both players used political connections to create difficulties for the opponent, and Kasparov publicly attacked the match officials and Karpov himself, even accusing him of using suspicious stimulants during the games.

The outcome of the match was decided only in the final game. FIDE, at Karpov's insistence, had reverted to the old twenty-four-game system for this match, including the proviso that the champion (i.e., Karpov) would keep the title in the event of a tie at five wins apiece. Had Karpov in fact won the final game, he would have remained champion. But Kasparov, as he said later, looked into his opponent's eyes and saw that he had lost his confidence. And so it was Kasparov who won the final game and the title.

Most grandmasters welcomed the change, praising the active, creative style of the new champion compared to that of Karpov, whom Botvinnik described as "an exploiter of other people's ideas." Even Kasparov said about him in the middle of the match: "If I'm correct, Karpov is trying to assimilate himself to my style and artistic approach. This is a kind of psychological victory for me."

One year later, the two met yet again. Despite Kasparov's protests—"Former chess champions have always had a significant psychological advantage in return matches, and it was not by chance that Botvinnik reconquered his title many times," he said—the match rules had provided for a rematch in the event the champion lost the title.

The match was to be split between London and

Leningrad, and the disputes started early: How many rest days should there be between the two halves of the match? Kasparov wanted only two days; Karpov, thirteen years older than his rival, wanted a week. Karpov got his way.

Due to the nervous tension, the quality of the games was generally low. After sixteen games Kasparov was ahead by three points, and it seemed the match would soon be over. But Karpov unexpectedly rebounded and won three games in a row. Kasparov accused one of his seconds of giving away his secrets, but objective analysis said that Kasparov's collapse was caused simply by overconfidence. Finally Kasparov, after turning on his draw-machine, won the match by one point.

Now that the rematch was out of the way, Kasparov was fair game for any challenger. And who should it be three years later but Karpov! And once again the psychological struggle started before the first game, when Kasparov's book, highly critical of Karpov, came out on the eve of the match.

This was another close fight. After losing game 23 Kasparov was in the uncomfortable position of having to win the final game to tie the match and retain the title—a draw would have given Karpov the match. But win it he did, saying later, "Karpov lost the game psychologically when he understood that the battle would not end in a short draw. He literally couldn't make moves."

Karpov's comment after the match was that "the intensity of the psychological warfare by Kasparov surpassed what challenger Korchnoi did against me between 1978–1981."

■ ■ ■

CHAPTER 6

PUTTING PSYCHOLOGY TO WORK FOR YOU

The preceding chapters reviewed the development of chess psychology and how some of the greatest players in history used it to their advantage. Now it's time to show you how to use this powerful weapon in your own games. Although much of what follows is aimed at the tournament player, the principles apply in all forms of chess competition and at all levels of play where your objective is to obtain the best possible result—that is, to win whenever you can, and to draw whenever you can't.

As you have seen, grandmasters make mistakes ranging from subtle positional inaccuracies to gross blunders—just as amateurs do. It is true that grandmasters, with their superior knowledge and refined technique, don't make quite so many of them, but even the greatest players are only human, and, just like amateurs, are subject to nervous tension, distraction, indecision, fatigue, intimidation, and all the other weaknesses of the human condition. And the more important the competition is, the more severe are the physical manifestations of tension and the greater the likelihood of error.

Many people who don't play chess think of it as a purely intellectual challenge. But if you've ever had the experience of suddenly realizing that you were about to lose an important game you thought you were winning, you know that your body reacted exactly as though your life were being threatened: your heart pounded, your pulse raced, your stomach did flip-flops, your skin broke out in a sweat. Such physical manifestations of stress are common to all players, and they can occur at any time, not only at critical moments.

Since your mental state can have such dramatic effects on your body, obviously your physical condition can affect your mental well-being. It follows that regular physical conditioning should be part of your overall chess training.

The importance of physical fitness in chess performance is a relatively recent insight. In Steinitz's day, for instance, chess was nowhere near as physically demanding as it is today, simply because Steinitz and his contemporaries played nowhere near as many games as we do. Even Capablanca, a player closer to our own time, played fewer than six hundred serious games in a career spanning three decades—an average of twenty games a year. An active grandmaster today plays between eighty and a hundred and twenty games every year. Even an amateur who enters just one weekend open tournament a month plays about sixty games a year—three times more games than Capablanca played.

Physical conditioning does not mean working out in a gym every day, but merely following a routine of reasonable physical exercise. The operative word is "routine." Botvinnik, the great pioneer of physical preparedness for chess contests, did no exercise beyond taking long walks, but he followed that regimen religiously. Whatever type of physical activity you choose should be practiced regularly. Exercise need not be strenuous, but to be effective it must be consistent.

Even if you can't bear the idea of exercising, at least you should avoid the bad habits that so many young people allow themselves to fall into: late hours, poor diet, bad hygiene, sloppy appearance. Feeling fresh and clean can do wonders for your self-confidence and can definitely improve your play. Eating lightly and abstaining from alcohol will help you stay alert.

It is absolutely essential to get enough sleep. Remember that a single playing session can last as long as five hours, sometimes longer, and in two-games-a-day open tournaments you may be sitting at the board for more than ten hours. And all that time you must be able to concentrate at top efficiency.

At weekend opens, young competitors often like to stay up half the night playing speed chess and then show up for their morning games unwashed, unshaved, and irritable due to lack of sleep. Far be it from me to begrudge a teenager the rare forbidden pleasure of staying up all night with his friends, but it's a dangerous habit, one that sooner or later will cost valuable points.

In 1951, when I was a young master in Budapest, my chess club played its regular match games on Sunday mornings. I would usually spend the preceding Saturday evenings dancing and enjoying the night life of a great city. On one occasion, when I was enjoying the evening far from where I lived but not very far from the chess club, I decided, with the wisdom of youth, that going home to catch a few hours' sleep made no sense. Instead, I stayed up the rest of the night with my friends and arrived at the club Sunday morning without having slept at all.

My opponent, a good positional player, had the white pieces. Considering my condition, I didn't think I could survive a long positional struggle, so I precipitated an early fight, an unusual strategy with the black pieces.

CLUB MATCH, BUDAPEST 1951
Queen's Gambit Declined

K. Korody	P. Benko
1 d4	d5
2 c4	c6

I rarely played this. Under the circumstances I would have welcomed the drawish Exchange Variation.

3 Nf3	Nf6
4 Nc3	e6
5 e3	Nbd7
6 Bd3	dxc4
7 Bxc4	b5
8 Bd3	Bb7

This was a fairly new idea then; the usual move was 8 . . . a6.

9 0-0	b4
10 Ne4	c5?!
11 Nxf6 +	gxf6

If 11 . . . Nxf6 12 Bb5 + would be very unpleasant. The text move ruins Black's kingside pawn formation but opens the g-file—which is why I entered this variation.

12 Qe2	Qb6
13 a3	

White wants to draw Black's c-pawn away from the center so he can safely play e4. If now 13 . . . bxa3 14 bxa3 and the open b-file will benefit White.

13 . . .	Bd6
14 axb4	cxd4
15 exd4	Rg8!

The critical position. If 16 Bxh7 Bxh2+ 17 Kxh2 Rh8 and Black regains the piece with advantage. White should play 16 Be4 to keep Black's bishop off the long diagonal, but apparently he doesn't sense the danger.

16 b5?

Saving the b-pawn but overlooking my threat. My opponent, wanting to play a positional game, couldn't adjust in time to the sudden tactical turn it was taking.

| 16 . . . | Qxd4! |
| 17 h3 | |

Obviously, 17 Nxd4 Rxg2+ 18 Kh1 Rxh2+ 19 Kg1 Rh1 is mate. The text move loses, too, but there is no good defense against 17 . . . Rxg2+ followed by . . . Qg4+.

| 17 . . . | Ne5! |

Now White has nothing better than taking the queen, but the game is over.

18 Nxd4	Rxg2+
19 Kh1	Rh2+!
White resigned	

If 20 Kxh2 Ng4+ 21 Kg1 Bh2 mate.

That game was hardly typical of my Sunday morning encounters: I lost some others due to lack of sleep. The point of this example is rather to show how external circumstances can affect the choice of opening. I needed a short game, so I picked a variation that would have led to a quick draw if my opponent were willing, and if not . . . well, you saw what happened.

There are no shortcuts to winning chess. You can use various ploys to induce an opponent to make mistakes (that's one of the main points of this book), but there's an ethical line you must be careful not to cross. It's okay, for instance, to create complications in your opponent's time pressure, but it's *not* okay to kick him under the table. In the first place, there is no satisfaction in winning a game through unsporting or unethical means. Second, a shady reputation is almost impossible to shake off. Third, you could do more harm to yourself than to your opponents.

An example was provided by the 1972 Fischer–

Spassky world championship match, during which Fischer showed up late for almost every game. Many young players, thinking that Bobby's lateness was calculated to upset his opponent, started emulating him. Actually, Bobby was late because of the constant crush of reporters and fans, those who followed his example only hurt themselves by sacrificing their own thinking time.

There's a psychological pitfall you should be aware of if you ever find yourself waiting for a tardy opponent. Don't overestimate the value of the extra time he is giving you, and don't be too eager to capitalize on it. If he came late on purpose, his idea was probably to give you a false sense of advantage so that you would err through overconfidence. The best way to handle that is to take the attitude that your opponent is only making things tougher on himself and that it is he, not you, who will have to worry about time pressure.

A talented American international master used to arrive late all the time to try to intimidate his opponents by showing his contempt for them. That attitude was undoubtedly one of the reasons he never obtained the grandmaster title despite his obvious gifts and his many years of trying.

Perhaps the best illustration of what can happen to a player who lets his opponent's lateness disturb his equanimity is Sammy Reshevsky's notorious loss to Fischer at the Interzonal tournament in Sousse 1967.

Fischer had been having a battle royal with the tournament directors over his schedule and had already forfeited two games. On the day he was scheduled to play Reshevsky, he was seen leaving his hotel with his luggage and getting into an airport taxi. But since he had not formally notified the tournament director that he was withdrawing, his clock was started at the scheduled time.

Reshevsky was seated at the board, happily con-
templating his good fortune as he waited for the required one hour to elapse for his opponent to be
forfeited, when suddenly, with only three minutes remaining, the news flashed through the hall that Fischer was coming! And then there he was at the board,
making his first move and pressing his clock.

Reshevsky, like everyone else in the room, was dumb-
founded. Unable to control his anger and surprise, he
lost his objectivity and failed to realize that he could
have exploited Fischer's lateness right in the opening.

SOUSSE 1967
Ruy Lopez

R. Fischer	S. Reshevsky
1 e4	e5(?)

This perfectly normal move is a psychological blunder, one of the costliest mistakes of Reshevsky's long
and illustrious career. Since Fischer had sacrificed almost half his allotted time, Reshevsky should have
chosen an opening that required difficult choices early
in the game and forced Fischer to use up thinking
time. The main line of the Ruy Lopez, which now
follows, runs to more than twenty moves and was one
of the most familiar of all openings to Fischer.

2 Nf3	Nc6
3 Bb5	a6
4 Ba4	Nf6
5 0-0	Be7
6 Re1	b5
7 Bb3	0-0
8 c3	d6
9 h3	h6

■ ■ ■ ■ ■

10 d4	Re8
11 Nbd2	Bf8
12 Nf1	Bd7
13 Ng3	Na5
14 Bc2	c5
15 b3	Nc6
16 Be3	cxd4
17 cxd4	Nb4?!

Up to Black's last move, all this was known theory. The equalizing method is 17 . . . exd4 18 Nxd4 d5 and if 19 exd5 Nb4. Maybe Reshevsky avoided it in fear of an innovation. Or did he forget the correct sequence because he was upset by the surprising turn of events?

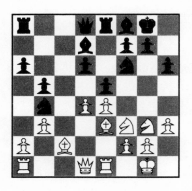

18 Bb1	a5
19 a3	Na6
20 Bd3	Qc7
21 Qe2	Qb7
22 Rad1	g6
23 Qb2!	

The queen goes to work on the long diagonal, giving Reshevsky new problems. "As his anger slowly grew his position worsened, and as his position worsened his anger grew," wrote Robert Wade in the tournament book.

23 . . .	Qb8
24 Bb1	Kh7?

Reshevsky overlooks a simple combination. Like it or not, he had to play 24 . . . Bg7.

25 dxe5	dxe5
26 Nxe5!	

How could Sammy miss a simple little trick like this? Now, having lost a pawn, he should get a grip on himself and try to make the best of his bad situation. But he loses his head and makes things worse.

26 . . .	Rxe5
27 Bf4	

Winning the exchange, for if 27 . . . Bd6 28 Rxd6.

27 . . .	Qb7
28 Bxe5	Ne8

Black is lost. When the game was adjourned at move forty-six, Reshevsky was so angry that he refused to resign, and during the second playing session he waited in the corridor until his time ran out. Thus his loss was officially—and ironically—recorded as a time forfeit.

Let that game serve as a dramatic object lesson in how off-the-board events can affect a player's judgment and concentration.

■ ■ ■

PSYCHOLOGY
IN THE
OPENING

In the summer of 1972, shortly before the Fischer–Spassky match, a drawing appeared on the cover of *Chess Life & Review* (now *Chess Life*), the magazine of the United States Chess Federation. It showed Spassky seated at a table with the two leaders of the Soviet government at that time, Brezhnev and Kosygin. On the table, next to a newspaper proclaiming Fischer's overwhelming victories over his most recent match opponents, is a stack of monographs dealing exclusively with openings beginning 1 e4. Brezhnev, looking worried, is asking Spassky, "But Boris, what if he *doesn't* play 1 P-K4?"

It was a prophetic drawing. Fischer, who had opened virtually every game of his life as White with the king pawn, began the sixth match game against Spassky with 1 c4. It was a devastating surprise, for although Spassky probably suspected that Fischer would deviate from 1 e4, he could not have predicted what he would play instead. With that one move, Fischer negated Spassky's preparations against 1 e4 and grabbed the psychological initiative, which he never relinquished.

Many people had feared that Fischer's reliance on 1 e4 would one day be his undoing, since it's easy for somebody to prepare a surprise when he knows what opening his opponent will play. The beautiful irony of the Spassky match was the way Fischer turned this "liability" into a crucial element of his victory. And Fischer says he doesn't believe in psychology!

Chess lore is rich in dramatic and amusing stories, but in the category of brilliant opening surprises few can equal Lasker's treatment of Capablanca in the St. Petersburg tournament of 1914.

It was the seventh round of the finals. Lasker and Capablanca were tied for the lead, and their game in that round would probably decide the winner of the tournament. This game was a must win for Lasker, since Capablanca was likely to score more points in his three remaining games than Lasker in his remaining two (Capa had already taken his free day and Lasker hadn't). By the same token, Capablanca, with the black pieces, could not afford to lose and had to play for a draw.

If you or I had been in Lasker's place, we would probably have played the opening aggressively, for the attack, for the win. Not Lasker.

Knowing that his opponent could not take risks and would be playing for a draw, he paradoxically chose one of the most drawish lines of the Exchange Variation of the Ruy Lopez. This variation promises White the better pawn structure and a slight edge in the endgame, but it also gives Black chances for active counterplay with his two bishops. Lasker's idea was that Capablanca, to avoid an inferior endgame, would be *forced* to play actively—precisely what he did not want to do.

Unsettled by Lasker's surprise, Capablanca played indecisively, missed his chance to take action, and lost. Lasker went on to win the tournament, half a point ahead of the great Cuban.

PREPARED VARIATIONS
AND OTHER NASTY SURPRISES

Opening surprises can take several forms. In addition to the opening switch (as in the Fischer game above) and the unexpected choice of opening (Lasker–Capablanca), the most common type of surprise is the prepared variation, which usually means a new move.

For an opening switch to be effective, you have to know what openings your opponent prefers. This is no problem for grandmasters, who play one another often and whose games are published all over the world, or for members of the same chess club, who usually know one another. In open tournaments, however, where dozens or hundreds of players congregate who have never met over the board, it is obviously impossible to prepare for a specific opponent. But a prepared variation in an opening that everyone plays can be very useful.

In the book *How to Open a Chess Game* (R.H.M. Press, 1973), Grandmaster Paul Keres explains the psychological effectiveness of a prepared variation:

A player who is presented suddenly with a new line must switch his train of thought—easier said than done. He tends to become unsure, even to lose the thread; rarely does he find the best countermove. And even if he does, he is still in an unequal position: his opponent knows the fine points of the system because of his home analysis, while the player facing the new variation for the first time must figure everything out over the board. It is this advantage that promises success to the player who can present his opponent with new problems.

The technique of analyzing an opening and working out new ideas is beyond the scope of this book (I recommend *How to Open a Chess Game,* especially the chapters by Keres and Larsen), but I can offer a few hints and warnings.

When you come up with a new idea, first test it in casual games or against your chess computer. That will give you a feel for the kinds of positions that are likely to arise, and some experience in handling them. As Keres wrote: "An innovation need not be especially ingenious, but it *must* be well worked out." Unless you know it thoroughly, you may find yourself in exactly the situation you were hoping to inflict on your opponent—adrift in an unfamiliar position.

Playing a prepared variation in a standard opening can be psychologically effective for several reasons: Your opponent, imagining danger where none exists, may play too passively; or he may try to punish you and play too aggressively; or he may spend so much time looking for a refutation that he will end up in time pressure.

Finding the right time to introduce an innovation is also important. When the result of the game doesn't matter or when your opponent is somebody you can beat with the normal moves, playing a new idea would just be wasting it. Remember: Once you've used it, it's no longer a surprise. As Bent Larsen wrote in *How to Open a Chess Game,* "Many players have such secrets and are willing to reveal them for a very reasonable price: one point!"

What should you do when you find yourself on the receiving end of an opening surprise? Here are two general pieces of advice:

1. Play sound developing moves! You can safely assume that your opponent has analyzed all the plausible moves at home, so searching for a sharp refutation over the board in an unfamiliar position would be asking for trouble. Besides, a sharp refutation may not even exist. One of the purposes of an opening surprise is to make you use up time on the clock. Sometimes you can't avoid that, but you can save time (and a lot of grief) by looking merely for healthy moves to keep the position in balance.

2. Don't get depressed or discouraged! The fact that your opponent has analyzed the position is no guarantee that his analysis or his judgment was correct. Remember this: If your opponent's idea were as good as the main line, it would *be* the main line.

The following games illustrate various types of psychological opening stratagems. The first game shows what can happen when you catch your opponent in a sharp opening that he doesn't know.

HUNGARIAN CHAMPIONSHIP, BUDAPEST 1950
Scotch Game

P. Benko	I. Molnar
1 e4	e5
2 Nf3	Nc6
3 d4(!)	exd4
4 Nxd4	Nf6

The other main line is 4 . . . Bc5, which is now usually answered by 5 Nb3. I once drew with Smyslov after 5 . . . Bb6 6 a4.

| 5 Nxc6 | bxc6 |
| 6 e5 | Ne4?! |

Few things are more unsettling at the start of a game than finding yourself in a sharp opening that requires precise move knowledge and it's an opening you haven't looked at in years, if ever. Although in general the defender's best policy when confronted with a surprise is to keep developing, there are times when general principles are of little use and you simply have to know specific moves. Like now.

The right move is the unlikely-looking 6 . . . Qe7. Although the queen blocks the bishop, the strong pressure it exerts on the pinned e-pawn is Black's best chance for equality. I have played the Scotch many times in my long career, and only rarely has my opponent known about 6 . . . Qe7. The move I saw most often was 6 . . . Nd5, after which I would get a good game with 7 c4.

It is precisely the fact that 6 . . . Qe7 looks wrong that makes the Scotch Game a good choice for White on occasion. Unless Black has studied this opening—and who studies the Scotch Game today?—he is unlikely to find 6 . . . Qe7 over the board. Even if he does, chances are he won't know how to follow it up.

Remember that although 6 . . . Qe7 is Black's best move here, it is by no means a refutation of the Scotch Game, and it should not deter you from playing this opening. Granted, the move gives Black counterplay, but with correct play Black gets counterplay in *every* opening.

One day you may find yourself playing one of these

old openings against somebody who knows it just as well as you do. Not to worry—you will be no worse off than in any other opening you both know. Most of these old openings are not unsound and have not been refuted; the reason they are rarely played is simply that they are unfashionable. That's why most players will not know them, a fact that will work in your favor if you take the trouble to learn them.

7 Qf3	Ng5

After 7 . . . Nc5 8 Bc4 Ne6 White soon castles and plays Bxe6, with practically a won game right in the opening.

8 Qg3	Be7

More than a quarter of a century after this game was played, the Scotch was still working for me: In the 1975 World Open, K. Dehmelt played 8 . . . Ne6, which is probably better than Molnar's move, but after 9 Bd3 d5 10 0-0 Bc5 11 Be3 Bxe3 12 Qxe3 I had an advantage in development and the better pawn structure, which I converted into a win.

9 Bd3	0-0
10 0-0	d5
11 f4	

Sometimes the attack is more important than development. Thanks to Black's knight maneuver starting with 6 . . . Ne4, White has been able to gain enough time to build up a strong attacking position. This must be exploited before Black consolidates and completes his development.

11 . . .	Ne4
12 Bxe4	dxe4
13 f5	Bh4

Black has to do something about the threat of f6 or Bh6. If 13 . . . Bc5+ 14 Be3.

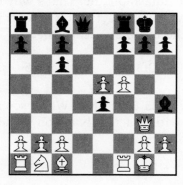

14 Qg4	Qd4+
15 Kh1	Be7
16 Bd2!	

Protecting the e-pawn with the threat of Bc3.

| 16 . . . | Rd8 |
| 17 Qg3 | Qc4 |

White has too many threats: f6, Bh6, even e6. Now, temporarily sacrificing a piece, he gains more time.

18 Na3!	Bxa3
19 Bh6	Bf8
20 Bxg7	Bxf5
21 Bxf8+	Bg6

After 21 . . . Kxf8 22 Rxf5 and 23 Raf1 Black's king is in trouble.

| 22 Bh6 | Qxc2? |

A mistake caused by time pressure. And the reason Black was in time pressure was that he had used up a lot of time finding his way in an unfamiliar opening.

Despite the opposite-colored bishops, White's threats of h4 and e6 give him a winning advantage.

23 Qg5	f5
24 Qe7	Bf7
25 Qf6	Black resigned

My opponent in the following game was a specialist in the old openings and had analyzed them in detail, so I knew I would have to play something else. My choice of opening was calculated to make him as uncomfortable as possible by forcing him to think strategically rather than rely on specific move knowledge.

LODZ 1949
Benko System

P. Benko	**Pytlakowski**
1 g3	

I've been playing this opening move most of my life, but it wasn't until 1962, when I beat both Fischer and Tal with it in the same tournament, that it was dubbed the Benko System.

Actually, it isn't a fully worked out system—it could hardly be that in view of Black's many possible replies and the myriad opportunities to transpose into other openings—but rather an attempt to avoid well-traveled opening paths. The idea is to preserve maximum flexibility so as to transpose into the line most appropriate to Black's play. This manner of handling the opening often works well against a booked-up opponent.

■ ■ ■ ■ ■

1 . . .	Nf6
2 Bg2	d6
3 d4	g6
4 Nf3	Bg7
5 0-0	0-0
6 c4	Nbd7

Black is trying to steer the opening into regular King's Indian lines. In later games (against Fischer and Tal, for example), I avoided this possibility by substituting Nc3 for c4. In this game, too, I took my opponent's nose out of the King's Indian book, though he didn't realize that until it was too late.

7 d5!?	Nc5

Twenty-six years later, in the 1975 United States Championship, I surprised Walter Browne with 7 d5 and he answered 7 . . . e5. After 8 dxe6 fxe6 9 Nc3 Nc5 10 Be3 Nce4 11 Nxe4 Nxe4 12 Qc2 Nf6 13 c5 White already had the better game.

Both Browne and my present opponent tried to stay in the King's Indian, as though 7 d5 were a perfectly normal move. Actually it *is* a normal King's Indian move, but this exact position never arises in the normal King's Indian Defense! The right reply is 7 . . . Nb6, which should equalize.

Often the best answer to a strange-looking move is another strange-looking move. Some players, when confronted with an unusual move in a familiar position, will try to continue as though everything were normal. In fact, simple development is usually the proper response. But the best policy, as always, is to find the strategy that best suits the particular circumstance.

8 Nd4	a5
9 Nc3	e5
10 dxe6	fxe6

Black can play 10 . . . Nxe6, but after 11 Nc2 (or 11 Ndb5) White is better because his e-pawn, still on e2, is not in the way of his pieces and can go to e3 or e4 according to the needs of the position. Black's capture looks logical because it seems to strengthen his center, but his center turns out to be immobile and to require constant defense.

11 Bg5!?	h6

Since 12 Bxf6 would be good for Black, the bishop retreats, apparently losing a tempo. More significant, however, is that this move weakens Black's kingside, especially the square g6.

12 Be3!	Ng4
13 Bc1	

White will play h3, Black's knight will retreat, and the bishop will return to e3, having *gained* a tempo.

13 . . .	c6
14 h3	Nf6

Black, intending . . . e5, avoids putting his knight on that square, though 14 . . . Ne5 would be safer.

15 Be3	Nfd7?!

If 15 . . . e5, as advertised, then after 16 Nf3 Ne6 17 Nh4 Black is in trouble. With so many pawns on the third rank, his position already looks suspicious.

16 Nf3!

Another retreat, this time with aggressive ideas of working against Black's weak d-pawn and g-pawn.

16 ...	Qe7
17 Nh4	Kh7
18 Qc2	Qf6
19 Rad1	e5

If 19 . . . d5 20 cxd5 exd5 21 Nxd5.

20 Ne4	Nxe4
21 Bxe4	

Black can no longer protect his g-pawn. The game concluded:

21 . . . Rd8 22 Nxg6 Kg8 23 Kg2 Nf8 24 Nxf8 Bxf8 25 f4 Qe6 26 f5 Qf6 27 g4 Kh8 28 h4! Qxh4 29 Rh1 Qe7 (If 29 . . . Qxg4+ 30 Kf2 followed by Rdg1; or 29 . . . Qf6 30 g5, etc.) 30 Bxh6 Kg8 31 Bxf8 Rxf8 32 Rh6 Rf6 33 Rdh1 Qg7 34 Rh8+ Qxh8 35 Rxh8+ Kxh8 36 g5 Rf8 37 Qd3 Rg8 38 Qh3+ Kg7 39 Qh6+ Kf7 40 Qh7+ Black resigned.

The opening of my game against Dr. Platz in the 1952 Budapest tournament had an interesting psychological element. Platz had lost nine games in a row and was desperate to salvage some measure of self-esteem. I decided to keep him off-balance by playing something new.

BUDAPEST 1952
King's Indian Defense

J. Platz	P. Benko
1 d4	Nf6
2 c4	g6
3 g3	Bg7
4 Bg2	0-0
5 Nc3	d6
6 Nf3	Nc6

At the time, this move was considered unsatisfactory because of 7 d5. I avoided the usual move, 6 . . . Nbd7 intending . . . e5, because of Dr. Platz's familiarity with it. After this game the 6 . . . Nc6 variation was reevaluated and became one of the main lines.

7 d5   Na5!?

The usual moves in this relatively rare line were 7 . . . Ne5 and 7 . . . Nb8. Judging by the expression on my opponent's face, he had never seen this move before and didn't think much of it. As far as I can tell, this was its first appearance in an international tournament. Nowadays it is the standard move, and 7 . . . Ne5 or 7 . . . Nb8 would be considered a surprise.

8 Qd3

Already justifying my opening strategy. Although this looks like a natural way to protect the c-pawn, the queen does not stand well here. Today the standard move is 8 Nd2.

8 . . .   c5

White must not be allowed to play b4.

> 9 0-0　　　　　　　a6

This is the point of 6 . . . Nc6 and 7 . . . Na5. Black prepares to play . . . b5 while his knight pressures the white c-pawn and his bishop on g7 rakes the long diagonal.

> 10 Rb1　　　　　　Qc7
> 11 b3　　　　　　　Bd7
> 12 Bd2　　　　　　Rfb8
> 13 a4

White tries to stop Black's freeing move . . . b5, but with both black rooks already on the queenside, that move now comes with even greater force. When you think you have prevented a good move by your opponent, it's depressing to see the move played anyway and with impunity.

> 13 . . .　　　　　　b5!
> 14 axb5　　　　　　axb5
> 15 cxb5?

If 15 Nxb5 Rxb5! 16 cxb5 Bf5, etc. White should have played 15 e4.

■ ■ ■ ■ ■

15 . . .   Nxb3!

Since White's other b-pawn will also fall eventually, his position is lost. Dr. Platz sacrifices the exchange in a desperate bid for counterplay, but that only makes things worse.

16 Rxb3	c4
17 Qb1	cxb3
18 Qxb3	Qc5
19 Rb1	Ra3
20 Qb4	Qxb4
21 Rxb4	Rxc3!
22 Bxc3	Nxd5

White resigned

The next game illustrates the consequences of an ill-chosen and badly concealed surprise.

Grandmaster V. Ragozin was a well-known Soviet theoretician. Although he had contributed important ideas in many openings, he was not much of a psychologist, as this game shows. With his second move, he put me on notice that he had something up his sleeve: Why else choose the Budapest Defense against a player raised and trained in the very city where that opening had been developed and deeply analyzed? Perhaps he expected this young Budapester (I was then twenty years old) to dive rashly into the wild complications for which this opening is known. If so, he made a serious miscalculation.

BUDAPEST–MOSCOW MATCH, 1948
Budapest Defense

P. Benko	V. Ragozin
1 d4	Nf6
2 c4	e5(?)

An unmistakable signal that something was up. If
you want to surprise your opponent, make sure it
really is a surprise!

3	dxe5		Ng4
4	Bf4		Nc6
5	Nf3		Bb4 +
6	Nbd2(!)		

Many wild variations may follow White's attempt
to hold the pawn with 6 Nc3 Qe7 7 Qd5. I was fairly
sure that Ragozin had cooked up something new in
that line, so instead of trying to keep the gambit pawn,
I aimed for the modest positional advantage White
gets in this opening if he does not strive for too much.

6	...	Qe7
7	a3	Bxd2 +
8	Qxd2	Ngxe5
9	Nxe5	Nxe5
10	e3	d6
11	Be2	Bd7
12	0-0	Bc6

White has the two bishops and the eventual c5
break. In fact, if 12 . . . 0-0, the immediate 13 c5! leads
to the isolation of Black's d-pawn because if 13 . . .
dxc5 14 Bxe5 Qxe5 15 Qxd7.

13	Rac1	0-0
14	Bg3!	

To prevent Black from winning a tempo with . . .
Ng6. Ragozin, finding himself in a rather different
type of game than he had expected, and facing the
prospect of a positional inferiority because of White's

two bishops, tries to create tactical complications. But his move is a tactical error.

14 ...	f5?
15 b4!	

Threatening b5 followed by Qd5+ winning the b-pawn, and also preparing the c5 break.

15 ...	Kh8
16 b5	Be8
17 c5!	

Black is in trouble. If 17 ... dxc5 18 Qd5, demonstrating the weakness of his queenside pawns and making White's bishop on g3 a powerhouse.

17 ...	Rd8
18 cxd6	cxd6

If 18 ... Rxd6 19 Qc3. Now Black will have to use most of his pieces to defend his weak, isolated d-pawn.

19 Rfd1	Bf7
20 Qd4	b6

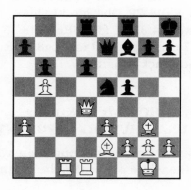

21 h4!

After 21 Bh4 Black has the defense 21 . . . g5. But
now the threat of h5 prepares Bh4 and h6.

21 . . .	Bb3
22 Rd2	Nf7
23 h5	Rd7
24 Bf3	Qf6

Ragozin would rather take his chances in an inferior endgame than endure the continuing pressure. I
followed the usual strategy of avoiding exchanges
when the opponent has a cramped position.

25 Qb4	Be6
26 Bc6	Rdd8

On 26 . . . Rc7 Black loses his doomed d-pawn, but
the text is no better.

27 Bh4	Qh6

If 27 . . . Ng5 28 Kf1 and 29 f4 wins. But not 28 f4?
Nf3+ (or . . . Nh3+). The game concluded:
28 Bxd8 Rxd8 29 Qh4 g5 30 Qd4+ Qg7 31 Bd5
Bxd5 32 Qxd5 f4 33 e4 f3 34 Rc7 Rf8 35 gxf3 Qf6 36
Qf5 Qxf5 37 exf5 Kg7 38 Rxd6 Kg8 39 Rdd7 h6 40 f6
g4 41 f4 and Black resigned.

HOW TO HANDLE A
DRAW-HUNGRY OPPONENT

Sometimes you run into an opponent who wants to
draw with the white pieces. Maybe it's the last round

and he doesn't want to risk a real fight because a win wouldn't improve his final standing but a loss would hurt it. Or maybe he is much lower rated than you and has no hope of winning but would be content with the small rating gain he would achieve with a draw. Or maybe he just isn't in the mood for a long struggle.

If he's a player of your own strength or better and has the white pieces, there isn't much you can do to avoid a draw (assuming that's what you want to do). But you can choose an opening that will make his job as hard as possible. For instance, he will probably want to set up a symmetrical pawn structure or exchange queens early, so you should avoid the French, the Caro-Kann, the Queen's Indian, the Queen's Gambit Declined, and other systems in which neither side gets winning chances if White chooses to simplify.

You can, however, play the King's Indian Defense, one of the few standard replies to the d-pawn opening that offer Black opportunities to outplay a draw-hungry opponent, even if queens are traded early. Here's an illustration.

HUNGARIAN CHAMPIONSHIP, BUDAPEST 1951
King's Indian Defense

J. Kapu	P. Benko
1 Nf3	Nf6
2 d4	g6
3 c4	Bg7
4 Nc3	0-0
5 e4	d6
6 Be2	e5

Theory considers it more promising to play this move first to give the queen's knight the option of going to c6. The "problem" with the text move is, of course, that it allows White to trade queens. That was fine with me: I have never felt uncomfortable without queens, and have been successful on both sides of this opening after early queen exchanges—especially against tacticians, who usually feel ill at ease without queens.

7 dxe5	dxe5
8 Qxd8	Rxd8
9 Bg5	Nbd7!?

The usual move is 9 . . . Re8, which I had played against Florian in an earlier tournament. Since that game had appeared in the newspapers and Kapu had presumably studied it, I added a new twist to avoid the possibility of prepared analysis.

10 0-0-0	Rf8!

The only move, strange as it seems. 10 . . . Re8 is answered by 11 Nb5, and 10 . . . h6 loses to 11 Bxf6 Bxf6 12 Nd5.

After playing 10 0-0-0 my opponent must have thought he was winning; his disappointment was obvious when he saw this move.

11 Nb5	c6
12 Nd6	Nc5

With his e-pawn under siege, White sees he has no advantage, so he tries to force a draw by trading pieces.

13 Bxf6	Bxf6
14 b4	Ne6
15 Nxc8	Rfxc8!

White seems to have achieved his aim: With bishops of opposite colors and his rook on the only open file, what does he have to worry about?

In fact, Black stands better because of White's overextended queenside pawns and exposed king, and the chance for a Black breakthrough on that side. Right now, for instance, Black's threat of . . . a5 is hard to meet. I was thinking about 16 Rd7 a5 17 c5 axb4 18 Bc4 b3! 19 Bxb3 Nxc5 20 Bxf7+ Kf8 and Black is winning.

| 16 Kb2 | a5 |
| 17 b5 | |

Abandoning the valuable c5-square, which Black's knight now happily occupies. But if 17 a3 axb4 18 axb4 Ra4 and . . . Rca8, and White is in pain.

17 . . .	Nc5
18 Bd3	Na4+
19 Kb3?	

The check was a little test to see how much my opponent saw in the position, and he failed. He saw the coming piece sacrifice but thought it led only to perpetual check. Actually, it leads to mate. Distasteful though it is, the only move is 19 Ka1.

| 19 . . . | cxb5 |
| 20 cxb5 | |

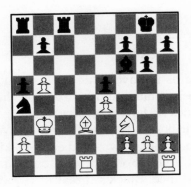

20 ...	Rc3 + !
21 Kxa4	Be7
22 b6	Rac8
23 Kxa5	

If 23 Kb5 Bb4! followed by . . . R8c5 + and . . . Ra3 mate.

23 ...	Ra3 +
24 Kb5	Rc5 +
25 Kb4	Rc2 +
26 Kb5	Rb2 +
White resigned	

Finally he saw 27 Kc4 Rb4 + 28 Kd5 Ra5 + 29 Bb5 Raxb5 mate.

REVERSED OPENINGS:
TRICKY TREATS FOR WHITE

Many grandmasters who used to play the King's Indian Defense at almost every opportunity lost their enthusiasm for it when White's play was strengthened in some important lines. Although it is less popular now than it once was, the King's Indian is still an active, fighting defense.

It stands to reason that the strategies that make the King's Indian Defense work for Black should make it work at least as well for White if he plays the moves that Black usually plays, since he gets the same position but a move ahead. The King's Indian Attack (also known as the King's Indian Reversed) does, in fact, work, and it has become almost as popular for White as the King's Indian Defense once was for Black.

The King's Indian Attack is a universal opening, effective against the Sicilian, the French, the Caro-Kann, and other defenses. Fischer started his career with it. I have had frequent success with it against such grandmasters as Robert Byrne, Pachman, Uhlmann, Csom, and others. The following game was played against the Icelandic grandmaster who later became president of FIDE.

REYKJAVIK 1957
King's Indian Reversed

P. Benko	F. Olafsson
1 Nf3	Nf6
2 g3	g6
3 Bg2	Bg7
4 0-0	0-0
5 d3	d5

Black accepts the invitation to play White's usual role in the King's Indian Defense.

6 Nbd2	c5
7 e4	Nc6
8 Re1	e5
9 exd5	Nxd5
10 Nc4	f6
11 c3	

The usual plan is 11 a4 to prevent . . . b5, then c3 followed by a5. But I was deliberately inviting . . . b5, which I thought would be a dubious move for Black because he is a tempo behind.

| 11 . . . | b5?! |

Although this drives White's knight from its good post, it weakens Black's c5 and his entire queenside. That was the point of my strategy. Now my plan was simply to work on Black's c-pawn.

12 Ne3	Be6
13 Nxd5	Bxd5
14 Be3	Qe7

The pawn would be weakened further by 14 . . . c4 because of 15 dxc4 followed by 16 Nd2, or first 15 a4.

15 Nd2	Rfd8
16 Bxd5	Rxd5
17 Qb3	Qd7
18 Qxb5	Rb8
19 Qa4	Rxb2
20 Nb3	

Provoking a simplification that emphasizes the weakness of Black's c-pawn. In view of the threat 21 Bc1, Black has little choice.

20 . . .	Nd4
21 Qxd7	Nf3 +
22 Kh1	Rxd7
23 Reb1	Rxb1 +
24 Rxb1	Rxd3
25 Kg2	Ng5

If 25 ... e4 26 Nxc5 and now Black can't take White's c-pawn because of 27 Nxe4 attacking two pieces.

26 Nxc5

Reestablishing material equality but with a bonus: White has a passed pawn and the more active pieces. And Black still can't take the c-pawn, this time because of 27 h4 Nf7 28 Rb8+ Bf8 29 Ne6 and wins.

26 ...	Rd8
27 Rb7	Rc8

Black could not save his a-pawn in view of the other threat, 28 Bxg5 followed by 29 Rxg7+ and 30 Ne6+.

28 Rxa7	Nf7
29 a4	

The rapid advance of this pawn decides the issue. The conclusion was: 29 ... f5 30 Ne6 Bf6 31 a5 Nd6 32 Rc7 Ra8 33 Rc6 Be7 34 a6 Ne8 35 a7 Bd6 36 Rxd6 Nxd6 37 Nc7 and Black resigned.

There are other openings which, though dubious or even downright unplayable as Black, are perfectly sound with colors reversed due to the extra tempo. These "reversed" openings have psychological advantages as well as theoretical ones. Your opponent may underestimate your position because of its bad reputation (in its usual form!) and will play too ambitiously. Or he may become confused or disoriented by a position that looks familiar but is subtly different. Many players, even very strong ones, can fail to appreciate the implications of White's extra tempo or the fact that as Black they are playing White's moves a tempo behind.

The unusual opening of the following game is a good illustration.

ZONAL TOURNAMENT, DUBLIN 1957
Philidor's Defense Reversed

P. Benko	C. H. O'D. Alexander
1 e4	e5
2 Nf3	Nf6
3 d3	

This is one way for White to avoid the drawish lines of the Petroff Defense. I also used to take my opponents out of the books with 1 e4 e5 2 Nf3 Nc6 3 c3 Nc6 4 d3 or 3 Be2 or even the immediate 3 d3. Why not?

3 . . .	Nc6

Although I have played 3 d3 many times, no one has ever tried 3 . . . d6 against me. That demonstrates one of the psychological advantages of reversed openings: Many players, thinking White is playing passively, will try to exact punishment by being overaggressive. Thus far my "punishment" has been to win virtually every game I have played with those moves against very strong opponents, including a renowned opening theoretician.

| 4 c3 | d5 |
| 5 Nbd2 | Be7 |

Black can't be too active. The aggressive 5 . . . Bc5 lets White gain an extra tempo (that is, an *extra* extra tempo, since he's already a tempo ahead of the normal lines) while expanding on the queenside with 6 b4.

6 Be2	0-0
7 0-0	h6
8 b4	a6
9 Bb2	Be6
10 a3	

White is planning to advance his c-pawn but first wants to see what Black does in the center. If Black advances his d-pawn, he will lose his e-pawn after White's c4 and b5.

10 . . .	dxe4
11 dxe4	

The pawn structure is balanced, but White's position is more flexible and more promising.

11 . . .	Nd7
12 c4	Bf6
13 c5	Re8
14 Nc4	Nf8
15 Qc2	Bg4
16 Rad1	Qb8!?

Of course, 16 . . . Qe7 is not safe because of 17 Ne3 threatening Nd5 or Nf5. Black's odd-looking move is part of a specific strategic idea: He wants to alleviate the pressure on his position by trading off White's knight on f3 and then maneuvering his own knight from f8 via e6 to d4, plugging the d-file. If that knight is captured when it gets to d4, Black must be prepared to recapture with a piece, not only to keep the d-file closed but also because recapturing with the e-pawn

would create a very weak pawn on d4. That's why the
more natural-looking 16 . . . Qc8 is not satisfactory, for
after 17 Ne3 Bxf3 18 Bxf3 Ne6 19 Bg4 Black can't play
19 . . . Ncd4 because of 20 Bxd4, forcing the pawn to
recapture.

17 Ne1!

Reserving the knight for the important job of controlling d4. It is very important to realize what your
opponent is up to so that you can frustrate his plans.

17 . . .	Bxe2
18 Qxe2	Ne6
19 Nf3	Nf4

Black, having been unable to carry out his plan,
now tries to create counterplay in another way, but
this is no problem for White. The black knight is in-
effective on f4 and soon leaves.

20 Qc2	Qc8
21 Ne3	

Defending against the threat . . . Nxg2, and now threatening to occupy d5 or f5.

21 . . .	Qe6
22 Qc4!	Rad8
23 Qxe6	fxe6

After 23 . . . Nxe6, either 24 Nd5 or 24 Nc4 is strong. Black's efforts to keep control of d5 have led to weaknesses elsewhere.

24 Nc4	Ng6
25 g3	Kf7
26 Rfe1	Ke7
27 Kf1	Rxd1
28 Rxd1	Rb8

Intending . . . b5. White was threatening Bc3 followed by a4 and b5, finally netting Black's e-pawn.

29 h4	h5
30 Ke2	b5
31 cxb6	cxb6
32 Rc1	

The immediate 32 Rd6 doesn't work: 32 . . . Rc8 33 Nxb6 Kxd6 34 Nxc8+ Kc7 and the knight is trapped.

32 . . .	b5
33 Na5!	Nxa5
34 bxa5	

White's queenside pawns are doubled but they aren't weak, since Black can't easily get at them. Black's a-pawn, however, is vulnerable to White's knight, which will soon be on its way to b4.

34 . . .	Kd7
35 Rd1+	Kc6
36 Bc3	Rb7
37 Ne1	Be7
38 Bb4	Rc7

If 38 . . . Bxb4 39 axb4 and White's knight gets a great square at c5.

39 Bxe7	Rxe7
40 Nd3	Rc7
41 Nb4+	Kb7
42 Rd6	Black resigned

A word of warning about reversed openings: If Black plays sensibly, these openings are no better for White than the regular lines. Their advantage lies in their unfamiliarity, in their surprise value, and in the possibility that your opponent will fall into the psychological trap of underestimating your position or overestimating his own. If you make the mistake of thinking that by surprising your opponent in the opening you have earned an automatic win, you deserve to lose.

■ ■ ■

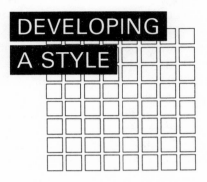

CHAPTER 8

DEVELOPING A STYLE

Many men, many styles; what is chess style but the intangible expression of the will to win.

—Aron Nimzovich

Although chess is, as Lasker wrote, above all a fight, in at least one way it bears comparison with the fine arts: It provides a form for the expression of individual style.

Style in the arts has two meanings. One refers to the characteristics of a certain nationality or historical period or school of thought. The other refers to the specific characteristics of a single artist. In music, for instance, although Haydn and Mozart both lived in the same region of central Europe at about the same time (the late eighteenth century) and both were leading representatives of the Classical style, their personal styles, as expressed in their music, are as different as their faces or their personalities.

In chess, too, we speak of style in a historical sense. The chess games of the nineteenth century were noted for their combinations, sacrifices, direct attack against the king, and, in the opening, a preponderance of kingside gambits. In the period between the two world wars, queenside openings became fashionable, as did the new "hypermodern" opening systems, in which direct contact between opposing forces was postponed until the middlegame.

After World War II, the dominance of Botvinnik and other Soviet players stimulated great interest in the so-called Soviet school of chess. That style, according to the Soviets themselves, was simply the confident, aggressive play of the nineteenth century wedded to the positional opening systems of the early twentieth century and supplemented by the psychological insights of Lasker (who is much admired in the Soviet Union), Alekhine, and Botvinnik.

If any single style predominates today, you might call it eclectic pragmatism if you wanted to impress somebody, or simply: the choosing or combining of various styles to produce optimum results. You could even say that there is no general style at all, only individual styles. Spassky and Fischer, for instance, and more recently Kasparov, belong to no school but are equally comfortable whether slugging it out tactically or maneuvering subtly for positional advantages.

A player's style is made up of many factors: character, attitude, education, talent, even genes. No one has ever demonstrated a correlation between personality and chess style, and in fact a player's personality is quite an unreliable guide to how he plays chess. We can easily recognize aggressive, cautious, reckless, timid, optimistic, materialistic, violent, and other styles of play; and we can certainly spot those same traits in the personalities of people we know. But it's a fact that many players who lead orderly, peaceful lives play brutal, violent chess, and vice versa: the turbulent personal lives of some famous players seem far removed from their logical, well-ordered play. Maybe that's what makes chess so attractive: It allows us to express a side of ourselves that we cannot or will not express in other ways.

Broadly speaking, there are two fundamental styles: defensive and offensive.

The defensive player is concerned above all with the safety of his own position. He advances slowly and methodically and takes no unnecessary chances, preferring to stifle his opponent's activity rather than to promote his own. He generally chooses "closed" openings—those beginning with 1 d4 or 1 c4 or sometimes 1 Nf3 or 1 g3.

The offensive player is overtly aggressive. His play is active and risky, and he tries to break through his opponent's defenses as quickly as possible without worrying too much about his own safety. He generally prefers "open" games—openings that begin 1 e4.

However, it would be a mistake to think that your opponent's choice of the e-pawn or the d-pawn tells you something useful about his style. Chess is not so simple. For example, Pillsbury, Spielmann, Marshall, and Alekhine, who were among the most aggressive players in the history of the game, all generally preferred 1 d4. The choice of opening move is a clue, but that's all.

We also recognize a tactical style and a strategic style, though here the distinction is not so clear. Strategists are long-range planners and maneuverers, and tacticians are usually more concerned with short-range combinations and precise calculation, but the two styles are by no means mutually exclusive. Petrosian, for instance, was a great strategist who by temperament disliked tactical situations, yet we could fill a book with his creative tactics and combinations.

Lasker attempted to fit all players into five style categories (which are paraphrased here):

1. The classical style: the player, using common sense, chooses plans according to scientific principles.
2. The automatic, or stereotyped, style: the player chooses moves from memory and without original creative thought.
3. The solid style: the player continually reinforces his position and waits for the opponent to err.
4. The come-and-get-me style, in which the player actively entices the opponent to attack prematurely.
5. The combinational style.

Lasker's list is much too short and is far from clear. His description of the classical style, for instance, is vague, since "scientific principles" is too broad a term. The "automatic" style is not really a style at all but merely an inferior method of play. There are simply too many variables for players to be usefully categorized in this way.

Moreover, a player's style can change. Most youngsters start out as aggressive attackers but later learn prudence and become more conservative. Two well-known examples are Maroczy and Keres, who began their careers as brilliant gambit players but in maturity developed positional styles. Even Tal, "the devil from Riga," has recently pulled in his horns somewhat and begun to play like a civilized human being.

Paradoxically, although every player has his own style—that is, leans toward particular patterns of play or prefers certain types of moves and positions—no player fits comfortably in any one category.

Style develops early. When a novice begins learning the game, he already exhibits certain natural stylistic tendencies: an eagerness to exchange pieces at every opportunity or a reluctance to exchange; aggressive pawn advances or slow, cautious play. These and other traits are as natural to him as his speech patterns, and, like his speech, will be refined as he gains knowledge and experience.

Chess is often just one of many games a child learns at home. All games to some extent train children to use their faculties and to develop skills. But chess, because it is not based on luck or chance, teaches the player above all that he alone is accountable for his actions. When he loses, he alone is to blame (that's why it hurts); when he wins, he alone gets the credit (that's why it feels so good).

A young player who shows talent for the game will eventually find a chess club or will begin playing in weekend opens or correspondence tournaments. This is where his chess education will really begin, for it is here that he will discover how little he knows about chess. The openings that succeeded so well against his father and little brother will be brutally crushed by players who have studied chess books, and endgames that he used to win so easily at home will suddenly become impenetrable mysteries.

If he is not discouraged—and he shouldn't be, for almost all strong players started out with similar ego-bruising experiences—he should continue his education by studying chess theory and playing over as many games by the great players as he can get his hands on. He will soon recognize the differences in their playing styles, and will begin to emulate players for whom he feels a natural affinity.

There is no reliable method of predicting how strong a player will become. Every grandmaster was once a beginner, the saying goes. But so was every duffer. One thing is clear: The younger a player is when he starts, the better are his chances of becoming a master.

My own early career approximately followed the above scenario. My father, who was not a serious player, taught me to play when I was eight, and I was soon beating him steadily. It was very nice for my ego, of course, that I could outdo my father at something— but it was not so nice for *his* ego, and it became harder and harder to coax him to play. I turned to my brother, who was about my own strength, but our rivalry became so bitter that chess was forbidden in the house in order to keep peace in the family.

I continued to play with my school friends, and in high school I competed in my first tournament. Later I joined a chess club, where I came in contact with older and stronger opponents, and within a year I was playing third board in club matches, a rather high place for an inexperienced player.

I was twelve when Emanuel Lasker died. The newspapers and magazines were full of stories about him, and his most famous games were printed everywhere. Of course I devoured the games, but the stories were no less intriguing: He played badly on purpose, they said. In studying his games I could see that he often had bad positions—but he won anyway! The paradox was irresistible, so of course he became my idol. As a teenager I read everything I could find about him and played over every one of his games countless times, trying to understand how he could defy the natural order of things and get away with it.

Though I hardly understood what I was doing, I tried to emulate him. Here's a game I played when I was fifteen against a candidate master in a club match. It is the earliest of my games that I have preserved.

BUDAPEST 1943
Ruy Lopez

P. Benko	N. Pesi
1 e4	

Like many young players, I always opened with the e-pawn. The closed systems, especially the ones with fianchettoed bishops on g2 or b2 (or g7 or b7), were deep mysteries to me. Chess literature was not plentiful then, and the only opening book I had was about the Ruy Lopez.

1 . . .	e5
2 Nf3	Nc6
3 Bb5	a6
4 Bxc6	

The old Exchange Variation, played under the influence of several famous Lasker games. This exchange, with the following trade of queens, suited my style anyway: I was already a good endgame player and had a strong interest in endgame studies.

4 . . .	dxc6
5 d4	

The usual move. This whole variation has never been particularly popular. In 1966, when Bobby Fischer played at the Havana Olympiad, he avoided this old queen exchange and castled instead. But when this game was played, 5 0-0 was considered very dangerous for White because of 5 . . . Bg4 followed by Black's offer to sacrifice the bishop after 6 h3 with 6 . . . h5. Fischer showed that White has nothing to fear in that line, and it enjoyed a vogue for a few years.

■ ■ ■ ■ ■

5 ...	exd4
6 Qxd4	Qxd4
7 Nxd4	Bd7
8 Nc3	0-0-0
9 Be3	Ne7
10 Rd1?!	

The usual move was 10 0-0-0. My idea was that this was, strategically, an endgame, and so the king should stay near the center to support the kingside pawn majority. That was stereotyped thinking, as Lasker might have chided. The exchange of queens does not automatically signify an endgame, and Black now shows that he has some attacking potential based on his two bishops.

10 ...	Ng6
11 f4?!	

Denying e5 to Black's knight but removing a potential defender of White's e-pawn. Black immediately starts working on this weakness.

11 ...	f6
12 Kf2	Bd6
13 Nde2	Rhe8
14 h3?	c5

Suddenly White's e-pawn is in trouble. Black will play ... Bc6.

15 Kf3	Bc6
16 Ng3	Nh4+
17 Kf2	g5!

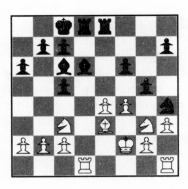

White's opening strategy is a failure. His king is unsafe and his center pawns unstable, and Black's two bishops are working at full strength—which pretty clearly explains why nobody plays the Exchange Variation this way.

I knew I was getting the worst of it. I asked myself what Lasker would do here, and I decided he would prefer tactical complications, however risky, to a long and painful death.

18 fxg5   fxg5
19 Nf5(!)

Of course not 19 Bxg5 because of 19 . . . Rf8 + winning a piece.

19 . . .   Nxf5
20 exf5   Rf8

Pesi now sat back with a satisfied smile, confident that he had avoided all the complications and would soon win a pawn while keeping the two bishops, which would win easily. But he gets a surprise.

| 21 g4!! | Bxh1 |
| 22 Rxh1 | |

In return for the exchange White has obtained a protected passed pawn and pressure against Black's kingside pawns. Since this variation is played so rarely, we don't often get to see one of its advantages for White: the possibility of rapidly mobilizing his kingside pawn majority by combinational means.

22 . . .	h6
23 h4	Be7
24 Ne4	

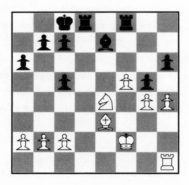

Black's promising position has evaporated, and now he has to deal with White's two connected passed pawns on the kingside. Perhaps he could have avoided losing, but it's very hard to adjust psychologically to fighting for a draw after having achieved a solid advantage.

24 . . .	Rh8(?)
25 f6	Rhf8
26 hxg5	hxg5
27 Bxg5	Rd5

A desperate try to save the game by giving back the exchange, but it's too late.

| 28 Ke3 | Rxg5 |
| 29 fxe7 | Black resigned |

After the game I felt I had gone through an initiation: Now I was a true disciple of Lasker! I had played "his" opening, achieved a suspicious if not downright inferior position, kept my head, played resourcefully, and won.

But it was clear to me that I could not expect always to survive such close calls. Objective analysis proved that my idea of exploiting White's kingside pawn majority as I did was naive. If I was going to improve, I would have to learn patience, and I would have to learn technique.

About a year after Lasker's death, Capablanca died, and a book appeared in Hungary containing three hundred of his games, many of them annotated by grandmasters. Although Lasker remained my idol, Capablanca's games taught me technique and enabled me, at age seventeen, to become a master.

I tell you all this to emphasize the importance of recognizing your own strengths and weaknesses and doing whatever is necessary to promote the former and get rid of the latter.

Experiment with many different openings. You'll find that certain openings or variations usually lead to the kinds of positions you prefer to play. Study those openings intensely and play them often. Don't worry too much about the results of the games; what counts is the training and the experience.

It is important to find a style that is natural for you yet also flexible enough to adjust to circumstances. If you like to build up your position slowly and you know your opponent is an aggressive attacking player, you could, for instance, switch to an aggressive style yourself. Attacking players hate to be on the defensive, and if your opponent isn't happy, you should be. Or you can aim for a dull, solid, drawish position without winning chances for either side. That would force your opponent to take dangerous risks if he wanted to make a fight of it.

The Hungarian grandmaster Istvan Bilek was a very colorful tactician in his younger days. We met several times over the board, and more than once I was bloodied by his sharp claws. After one such experience I vowed that henceforth I would take the initiative against him at the first opportunity and never give him a chance even to think of attacking.

BUDAPEST 1954
Caro-Kann Defense

P. Benko	I. Bilek
1 e4	c6
2 Nf3	d5
3 Nc3	dxe4
4 Nxe4	Nf6
5 Nxf6 +	exf6

Black can play 5 . . . gxf6 followed by castling on the queenside (the Nimzovich Variation, also known as the Bronstein/Larsen Variation). The overall idea is the same as the text: Black gets free play and attacking chances as compensation for his weakened kingside pawn structure.

6 Bc4	Bd6
7 Qe2 + (!)	

Since Black's pawn structure meant that in an endgame he would have to defend an inferior position, I knew that Bilek would not permit the exchange of queens after 7 . . . Qe7. But retreating his bishop is a costly loss of time and increases White's initiative.

7 . . .	Be7!?
8 0-0	0-0
9 Re1	Bd6
10 d4	Bg4
11 h3	

In *Understanding the Caro-Kann Defense* (R.H.M. Press, 1981), Jack Peters writes of a similar position: "Although there are no targets in Black's position, he stands worse. He has less space, no direct threats, an inferior pawn structure for the endgame, and no good square for his queen bishop."

11 . . .	Bh5
12 g4!?(!)	

This committal move exposes White's kingside somewhat, but it breaks the pin and signals the beginning of White's attack. More significantly, it put Bilek in the (for him) unpleasant situation of having to play defensively.

12 . . .	Bg6
13 Nh4	Nd7
14 Nxg6	hxg6
15 Qf3	Nb6
16 Bb3	a5
17 c3	a4
18 Bc2	g5

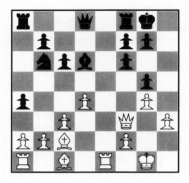

Black's idea is to blockade the kingside while preparing to station a piece on f4. White must play sharply.

19 h4!   g6

Black is understandably reluctant to go into 19 . . . gxh4 20 g5 fxg5 21 Qh5 f5 (if *21 . . . g6 22 Bxg6 fxg6 23 Qxg6+ Kh8 24 Qh6+ Kg8 25 Re6* wins) 22 Bxg5 with good attacking chances for White.

20 h5

White tries to pry open the diagonals for his bishops. Black tries to keep them closed.

20 . . .	Kg7
21 hxg6	fxg6
22 Qd3	f5
23 Re6!	

White must keep the initiative at all cost. There is no time to worry about developing the queenside.

23 . . .	Qd7
24 gxf5	Rxf5

My plan was to meet 24 . . . gxf5 with 25 Qe3, after which Black would be unable to prevent further incursions. Another possibility after 24 . . . gxf5 was 25 d5 followed by Qd4 + .

25 Qe2	Rf6
26 Rxf6	Kxf6
27 Qf3 +	Kg7
28 Bxg5	

Black's play has not been very inspiring, and it's hard to believe that the Black forces were being led by a famous tactician. But you can't really blame Bilek, since he was not being allowed to play in his natural style. As a result, White has won a pawn while keeping his two bishops and the attack.

28 . . .	Rf8
29 Qg2	Qe6

There is no time to activate the knight because White was threatening Bh6 + (*29 . . . Rh8 30 Bf6 +*).

30 Bd2	Rh8

Trying to organize effective counterplay. If 30 . . . Nc4 31 Re1 and 32 Bc1.

31 Re1	Qf7
32 Qg4	Bh2 +
33 Kg2	Bd6
34 Kg1	Bh2 +
35 Kf1	

White repeated moves to gain time on the clock. Black repeated moves because he had nothing constructive to do.

35 . . .	Nc4
36 Bg5	Bd6
37 Re6	Rh2
38 Rxg6 +	Kh8
39 Bf6 +	Black resigned

It is not always possible, even if you have the white pieces, to be the first to attack. Sometimes you simply don't get the right sort of position. But there is another way of dealing with an aggressive attacking player: enticing him to attack unsoundly so that when his attack fails your counterattack will win. This is risky—what if his attack succeeds?—but it can be effective against an opponent desperately seeking a win.

Laszlo Szabo was among the leading tacticians of his generation and was responsible for many beautiful games. When this game was played, he was thirty and in his prime.

HUNGARIAN CHAMPIONSHIP, BUDAPEST 1947
Nimzo-Indian Defense

P. Benko	L. Szabo
1 d4	Nf6
2 c4	e6
3 Nc3	Bb4
4 e3	0-0
5 Bd3	d5
6 Nf3	c5
7 0-0	Nc6
8 a3	Bxc3

9 bxc3	dxc4
10 Bxc4	Qc7
11 Bd3	e5

This has become one of the most popular lines of the Nimzo-Indian, but in 1947 it was fairly new. Knowing little about it, I could only hope my moves were the right ones.

12 dxe5	Nxe5
13 Nxe5	Qxe5
14 Qc2	Re8
15 f3	

Stopping ... Ng4 and preparing to mobilize White's central pawn majority.

15 ...	Bd7
16 e4	c4
17 Be2	Qc5+
18 Kh1	Bc6

White's queen bishop cannot be effectively developed on f4 (because of ... Nh5), and it obviously can't go to e3, which would be its ideal square. It could go to a3 after White plays a4, but that's not where it belongs. In addition to White's development problem, Black has some pressure against the e-pawn and the possibility of a piece sacrifice there for two pawns and a mating attack.

All this would seem to make it hard for White to set up his pieces effectively. Hard, yes—but not impossible. White does have the two bishops, after all, and with his next move he prepares to throw Black on the defensive.

19 Rd1!!

Strategically, an excellent move. My plan was to answer 19 . . . Rad8 with 20 Rd4!, preparing Be3. If 20 . . . Rxd4 21 cxd4 Qxd4 22 Bb2, White wins back the pawn and gets two beautifully working bishops.

Tactically, the move is provocative, since it removes a potential defender from the area surrounding the king.

Psychologically, it lures Szabo into an unsound sacrifice. Szabo, like all aggressive players, does not like to defend, and I hoped this move would tempt him to try something. Luckily for me, he remains true to his style.

19 . . .	Bxe4?!
20 fxe4	Nxe4
21 Rd4	Qf5

White's position looks critical. Black's main threat is to win the queen with . . . Ng3+ or . . . Nf2+. If 22 Kg1, Black ends the game with 22 . . . Qf2+ and mate in a few moves. If 22 Qb2 or 22 Qa2, still 22 . . . Qf2 is

very strong. The plausible sacrifice 22 Rxe4 is met by
22 . . . Qxe4 23 Qxe4 Rxe4 24 Bf1 Re1 25 Kg1 Rd8 26
Bb2 Rxa1 27 Bxa1 Rd1 28 Bb2 Rb1 and the bishop is
trapped.

22 Ra2!!

The only defense. It looks strange, since Black's
threats are based on the weakness of White's first rank,
and maybe that's why Szabo didn't see it when he was
calculating his sacrifice.

If now 22 . . . Qf2 23 Rd1 (best; either *23 g3* or *23 g4*
also defends, but less safely) 23 . . . Qh4 24 Be3 Ng3 +
25 Kg1 Rxe3 26 hxg3 and White should win. Szabo
decides to increase the complications, but now they
amount to no more than tricks.

22 . . .	Nf2 +
23 Kg1	Nd3
24 Bf4	Rad8

Black can try 24 . . . Rxe2 25 Qxe2 Nxf4, but after
26 Qe4 or 26 Qf1 Black cannot survive.

25 Rxd8	Rxd8
26 Be3	Qe4
27 Qd2	h6
28 Ra1	Rd6

Black's brief attack has fizzled. The last dimly glow-
ing ember, 28 . . . Re8, is snuffed out by 29 Bxd3,
leaving Black a piece down without sufficient compensation. The rest of the game was played in time
pressure, which accounts for the less than perfect
technique.

29 Bf3	Qe7
30 Bd4	b5
31 Be2	Re6
32 Bxd3	cxd3
33 Rf1	

A player in time pressure (as I was) tends to make unnecessarily noncommittal moves in fear of overlooking something. A quick resolution was possible after 33 Qxd3 Re1+ 34 Rxe1 Qxe1+ 35 Qf1. The actual end took a little longer:

33 . . . Qxa3 34 Qxd3 a6 35 Qf3 Qe7 36 Qa8+ Kh7 37 Qa7 Qxa7 38 Bxa7 f6 39 Bc5 a5 40 Rb1 b4 41 cxb4 axb4 42 Rxb4 Rc6 43 Be3 Rc7 44 Ra4 Kg6 45 Ra7 Rxa7 46 Bxa7 and Black resigned.

Understanding your own natural tendencies can help you become a better player, and knowing something about your opponent's style can sometimes give you an extra edge—not a decisive edge, perhaps, but any edge is better than none at all.

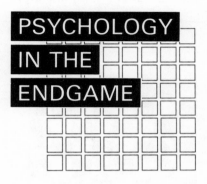

CHAPTER 9

PSYCHOLOGY
IN THE
ENDGAME

It ain't over till it's over.
—Yogi Berra

The endgame is often thought of as the technical phase of the game when the advantages accumulated during the opening and middlegame are cashed in. But at no time can chess be reduced to mere routine. Few endgames are as clearly won or drawn as we would like them to be, and no one's technique, save that of a world champion, is so flawless as to guarantee the desired result. The hardest game to win, as many broken-hearted players will attest, is a won game.

As long as the possibility of error exists, there exists also a psychological element, for most errors are psychological in origin. In the endgame, the most common errors, besides those resulting from ignorance of theory, are caused by either impatience, complacency, exhaustion, or all of the above. Not even the greatest masters are completely immune to those human failings.

Impatience, for example, is typical of young play-

ers; but look at what happened to Sammy Reshevsky
in the 1964 United States Championship:

S. Reshevsky

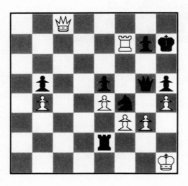

L. Evans

After errors on both sides in the opening and middlegame, Reshevsky reached this clearly winning position, with an extra piece and virtually a forced mate
in a few moves. He was probably wondering why
Evans didn't resign—but he should have been thinking about the position on the board.

48 . . .   Qxg3??

The win is 48 . . . Qg6 49 Rf8 Qe6! 50 gxf4 Re1 + 51
Kh2 Qa2 + and mates, as Evans pointed out. He now
produces the most infamous swindle of modern times.

49 Qg8 + !!   Kxg8
50 Rxg7 + !

And only now did Sammy see that he had to allow either perpetual check or stalemate.

Complacency—thinking that the result of the game is a foregone conclusion and that it doesn't matter whether you play this move or that one—is just as dangerous as impatience. Granted, sometimes it really doesn't matter which move you play, as long as it's a reasonable one. But never allow yourself to forget that your opponent is just waiting to catch you napping. Portisch was painfully reminded of that in the 1976 Interzonal tournament in Biel.

L. Portisch

B. Larsen

This was the adjourned position of a game between the two tournament leaders. White stands slightly better, but Black, thanks to his well-placed knight, should be able to hold. If White ever plays Bxd4, the opposite-color bishops will guarantee a draw.

Judging by his play after the game was resumed, Larsen had not found a decisive continuation during his adjournment analysis. So he tries to improve his position in tiny increments, using little tricks to wear down his opponent—a technique we will see again in this chapter.

42	Ra3	Rb8
43	Ra7	Nb5
44	Ra1	Nd4
45	Ke1	Kg8
46	Ra7	Nb5
47	Ra2	Kf7

Larsen has not been able to make use of his only open file. Now he tries to make progress by bringing his king to the queenside, but this leads to an improvement in *Black's* position.

48	Ke2	Ke6
49	Ke3	Nc7
50	Kd3	Rd8 +
51	Kc2	Nb5
52	f3	Nd4 +

While White has made no real progress, Black's position has improved, which undoubtedly convinced Portisch that White could not win. He was right, but you can *never* relax against Larsen.

53	Bxd4(!)	Rxd4?

Larsen is a very shrewd psychologist. He could have taken the knight at any time, but he didn't because Black had only one way to recapture, and it led to a draw. Now, with the black rook on the d-file, Portisch has a *choice* of recaptures. Larsen's nasty idea—which of course risked absolutely nothing—was to give Portisch a chance to go wrong with an "active" possibility that he didn't have before. Portisch, under the spell of the foregone conclusion, allows himself to be seduced, to his eternal regret. With the sober 53 . . . exd4 he would have secured the good e5-square for his bishop, a passed pawn, and a certain draw.

| 54 Kb3 | Be7 |
| 55 Ra7 | |

The third visit by the rook to a7, and this time it's effective. Black has no counterplay (as he would have had after *53 . . . exd4*), for if 55 . . . b6?! 56 b5!. So he is forced to defend passively, and he quickly finds his position untenable.

| 55 . . . | Rd7 |
| 56 g4! | |

Pushing the rook to a bad spot by threatening Bf5 + .

| 56 . . . | Rc7 |
| 57 Ra8 | |

Threatening to win the h-pawn.

| 57 . . . | Kf7 |
| 58 Rb8 | |

The game was adjourned here for the second time, and Black later resigned without resuming play. He can't defend against White's threats of Bf5-c8 and Ka4-a5-b6.

In the endgame, we are not concerned with developing pieces, opening lines for attack, safeguarding the king, or with any of the other themes belonging to the opening and middlegame. The business of the endgame is maneuvering to control critical squares, advancing or blockading passed pawns, preparing a breakthrough by the king, or exploiting the subtle superiority of one piece over another.

This kind of play demands just as much alertness and attentiveness as the other phases, but because of the endgame's slower pace and lack of action, alertness and attentiveness are sometimes in short supply. To make matters worse, endgames are often critical. An inaccuracy in the opening or middlegame is not necessarily fatal—with a little cooperation on the opponent's part, it may later turn out to have no ill effects at all. But in the endgame, even a slight mistake can make the difference between winning and losing. There is no "later."

It's exhausting to have to stay alert for long periods of time when nothing much is happening and after already having struggled through a long game. Exhaustion leads to impatience. If we have the advantage, we can be in a hurry to put the opponent out of his misery and post the win. If we have an inferior endgame, especially one that is not actually lost but requires long, patient, careful defense, it is all too easy to lose heart and to be too willing to get it over with.

Patience is the most valuable trait of the good endgame player. This explains why so few young masters play endgames well.

My game with Barcza in the 1950 Hungarian Championship is a good demonstration of what can happen when one player is patient and the other isn't.

G. Barcza

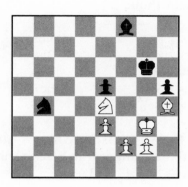

P. Benko

This was the adjourned position. Although White is a pawn ahead, analysis revealed no immediate win or even a clear win at all. But it was obvious that sooner or later I would have to advance my pawns to create a passed pawn—two passed pawns, if possible. But first I would have to drive Black's pieces into positions where they couldn't stop my pawns. This I would do by threatening to penetrate with my king, attacking Black's isolated pawns and forcing favorable exchanges.

Frankly, I was hoping that Barcza would find all this so unbearable that he would become impatient and make a mistake.

When playing over endgames between grandmasters, we often see what appears to be aimless shifting of pieces. But it isn't really aimless. Sometimes players need to gain time on the clock by repeating the position, but most often its purpose is to wear down the opponent psychologically. It works more often than you might think.

41 Kf3	Nc2
42 Ke2	Bb4
43 f3	Ba5
44 Nd6	Bc7
45 Be7	Nb4

If 45 ... Bxd6? 46 Bxd6, White is attacking the e-pawn and threatening to trap Black's knight; e.g., 46 ... Kf5 47 Kd2 Na1 48 Kc3, etc.

46 Ne4	Nd5
47 Bh4	Bb6
48 Bf2	Ba7
49 Kd3	Bb6
50 Nd6	Kf6
51 Nc4	Bc7
52 Bh4+	Ke6
53 Bg5	Nb4+
54 Kc3	Nd5+
55 Kd3	

For a while it seemed that White's king was trying to creep around the queenside to break into Black's position. That was not White's main plan, however, but a means of drawing Black's pieces away from their best posts.

55 ...	Nb4+
56 Ke2	Kf5
57 Be7	Nc6

58 Bh4	Ke6
59 Nd2	Bd8
60 Bf2	Ne7
61 Nf1	Nf5
62 e4	

White's true plan is revealed. Now Black's knight must go to a passive square to protect his h-pawn. If 62 . . . Nh4 63 Bxh4, leading to a clearer White advantage, since with Black's e-pawn on a dark square, his remaining piece would be inferior to White's knight. In my analysis of the many variations leading from the adjourned position, I always kept a careful eye on the possibility of this exchange.

62 . . .	Ng7
63 g3!	

White's only practical winning plan is to mobilize the extra pawn, and I now prepared to advance my f-pawn. Should Black capture it, White would get connected passed pawns; if not, White could play either fxe5 or f5 and try to work out the win with his passed pawn.

63 . . .	Bc7
64 Ne3	Kf7

Not 64 . . . Bb6? 65 Nf5!.

65 Nd5	Bb8
66 Be3	

There's no hurry to play f4—let Black worry about it a little longer! Besides, 66 f4 h4 could lead to too many pawn exchanges. If White is left with only a single pawn, Black could find a chance to give up a piece for it and achieve a theoretically drawn position.

| 66 . . . | Ke6 |
| 67 Bg5 | Nf5 |

White's slow maneuvering pays off as Black becomes impatient to get his knight to a more active position. The following exchange greatly simplifies White's task. The outcome of the game would have remained in doubt if Black had kept his shirt on.

| 68 exf5 + | Kxd5 |
| 69 Be7! | |

Temporarily preventing Black's king from getting back to the kingside and also clearing a path for the passed pawn; e.g., 69 . . . e4 70 fxe4 + Kxe4 71 f6. Since White will create a second passed pawn, Black's position is hopeless. If 69 . . . Kc6 70 Ke3 followed by Ke4, seriously threatening the e-pawn.

69 . . .	Ba7
70 g4	hxg4
71 fxg4	Kc6
72 g5	Kd7
73 Bb4	e4
74 Bc3	Bc5
75 g6	Ke7
76 Bg7	Kd7

Zugzwang: Black has nothing but bad moves. His Bishop can't leave the a7-g1 diagonal because of 77 Ke3, or the f8-a3 diagonal because it needs to watch the f-pawn's queening square.

| 77 Bh6 | Black resigned |

If 77 . . . Ke7 (to stop the g-pawn) 78 Bg5 + Kf8 79 f6 Kg8 80 Bh6 followed by f7 +, etc.

It's seldom possible to know for certain what was in a player's mind during a game. That's why it's very difficult to annotate somebody else's games and tell the truth about what was going on. The annotator has nothing to go on but the moves—not the tension, the exhaustion, the clock, the emotion, the toothache— just the moves.

That has never stopped anybody from annotating other people's games. But you shouldn't wonder why you see such terms as "inexplicable error" and "mysterious move." Nothing is inexplicable or mysterious if you know where to look for the answers. Take the following endgame, which was not appreciated by those who annotated it.

CANDIDATES' TOURNAMENT, BLED 1959

V. Smyslov

P. Benko

This was the adjourned position, with White to move.

As in the previous example, I had an extra pawn, but here I had even better winning chances. Analysis failed to show a clear or immediate win, however, so I decided to avoid committing myself to any specific plan at first.

Black has to watch out for White's pawn push g4 and must be ready for a general White pawn advance on the kingside. He has to make sure his c-pawn can always be adequately protected. He must prevent White's king from penetrating.

I could take my time deciding which of these long-range threats, alone or in combination, would be most effective. First I wanted to see how Smyslov prepared to meet them.

In the tournament book, Gligoric wrote: "White has

a winning endgame, not only because he has an extra pawn but also because his king is actively placed. On resumption of play Benko does not immediately find the way to win. His first moves do not lead to his goal, but they definitely show up all the weaknesses in Black's position."

It's easy to see that White has a solid advantage, but not at all easy to prove that it's an absolute win in a practical game—especially against Smyslov, a former world champion and a superb endgame player. Had this position been an adjourned game of Gligoric's, he would certainly have spent all night analyzing it, as I did, and he would not then have stated so categorically "White has a winning endgame."

42 Kc3

Apparently planning to penetrate via b3, a4, and a5, and then to push the b-pawn.

42 . . .   g5

Black cannot activate his king by 42 . . . Kd5 because of 43 Ne8. His best policy is probably to wait, but White does have actual threats, so he can't wait forever. He decides to reduce the potency of White's possible kingside advance by trading a pair of pawns, which also sets up White's f-pawn as a potential target if White gets careless. But Smyslov's pawn move leads to another kind of problem for both sides, as we will see.

43 Kd4

Now that Smyslov has changed the situation on the kingside, White's king returns to the center.

43 ...	gxf4
44 gxf4	Ba6

If 44 ... Bh3 45 f5+ is still good: 45 ... Bxf5 46 Nxf5 Kxf5 47 b5! cxb5 48 c6 Ke6 49 Kc5 and wins.

45 f5 +	Kd7
46 Nc4	Bb5
47 Kc3	Ba6
48 Kb3	Bb5
49 Nd6	Be2
50 Kc3	

Although White seemed to be trying to penetrate on the queenside (which he could now do with 50 Ka4), that was not his real threat. Black would put his king on c7 and his bishop on d3, and White could make no further progress on that side. If White played b5 he would allow Black's king to become active via c6 (after ... cxb5). Then Black could even sacrifice his bishop for White's last queenside pawn, and with White's king stranded on the queenside, Black could walk his king to the kingside and eliminate White's remaining pawns, drawing the game.

This general scenario helps to explain Smyslov's 42 ... g5 and 43 ... gxf4, which separated White's pawns and made them easier to attack. When Gligoric wrote, "His first moves do not lead to his goal," he forgot the old chess adage, "The threat is stronger than the execution." (See Chapter 13.) White's sham threat to penetrate on the queenside provoked Black's pawn action and made it possible for White to penetrate on the *kingside*.

Black's prospects are anything but pleasant. He cannot undertake any action but can only try to meet White's threats as they arise. Now we see another example of the wearing-down technique.

50 . . .	Ke7
51 Nc4	Kd7
52 Ne3	Ke7
53 Nc2	Kd7
54 Nd4	

A new square for the knight, new worries for Black.

54 . . .	Bf1
55 Kd2	Bc4
56 Ke3	Bf7
57 Kf4	Bc4
58 Kg4	Bf7
59 Kh4	

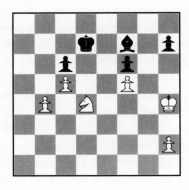

| 59 . . . | Kc7? |

All chess players have painful memories. One of mine is a game I played against Korchnoi in Belgrade

1964. I had a slightly inferior endgame that probably should have been drawn, but Korchnoi kept torturing me with little threats until finally, exhausted and exasperated, I made a losing mistake. Another such scar was inflicted by Geller at an Olympiad. I remember thinking at the time, "The hell with the result—let's just end this torture!"

Smyslov may have been having similar thoughts at this point. He probably saw that if White tried to win the h-pawn by Ne6+, Nf8, and Nxh7, the knight would be trapped, so he decided it wasn't a threat. But he should have looked a little deeper. The reason he didn't was that he was exhausted by his long, unpleasant defense and wanted it to end.

The English chess writer Harry Golombek, who also wrote a book about this tournament, pointed out here: "The long and rather monotonous shifting around the pieces in which Benko has indulged is now relieved by an excellently played ending. With his next move Benko deliberately immolates his knight in order to force a won pawn ending." Golombek, like Gligoric, missed the psychological component of this game: the "monotonous shifting" that exhausted my opponent and made possible the "excellently played ending."

Black should play 59 . . . Be8 to keep the fight going. If White tries 60 Ne2 Ke7 61 Ng3, then not 61 . . . Kf7 62 Ne4 Ke7 63 Nd6 Bd7 and the Bishop has no moves, allowing White's king to maneuver freely, but 61 . . . Bd7 62 Kg4 (to protect the f-pawn) followed by Ne4-d6 and White still has a long row to hoe.

60 Ne6 +   Kd7

If 60 . . . Kc8 61 Nf8 Bg8 62 Kh5 and wins.

61 Nf8 + !	Ke7
62 Nxh7	Bg8

The knight is trapped, but that's a small price to pay for a full point. The possibility of this "sacrifice" was not an over-the-board inspiration, as Gligoric and Golombek assumed, but had been prepared in various forms during my adjournment analysis after move 41.

63 Ng5!	fxg5 +
64 Kxg5	Kf7
65 h4	Kg7
66 f6 +	Kf8
67 h5	Bc4
68 Kf4	Kf7
69 Ke5	Bd3
70 h6	

The threat is 71 b5, against which Black has no defense except to allow White's king to penetrate.

70 . . .	Kg6
71 Ke6	Bc4 +
72 Ke7	Bd5
73 f7	Bxf7
74 h7	Black resigned

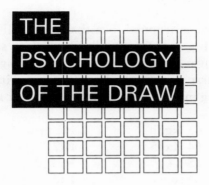

CHAPTER 10

THE PSYCHOLOGY OF THE DRAW

The psychological aspect of the game—understanding and exploiting the strengths and foibles of one's opponent—can be, as we have seen, a powerful weapon in the hands of those who know how to use it. At no time is this more true than in the circumstances surrounding the offer of a draw. Players must take into account such factors as their respective strengths, their standings in the tournament, their previous results against each other, their next opponents, their results in the previous round, their styles, their ages, the time on the clocks, and so on—and, of course, the position on the board.

There are many different kinds of players, and they don't all feel the same way about draws. Some will accept a draw at any time against almost anyone. Others will want to keep playing as long as they feel safe but will gladly extend their hand at the first sign of danger. Players who don't like to draw early in a tournament may be happy to split the point in the later rounds. And there are those who never draw at all if they can help it, following the example of Bobby Fischer.

Fischer was known for his abhorrence of draws even as a teenager. Only when a position was devoid of even the tiniest possibility of active play would he accede, unhappily, to a draw. In his view, a game of chess consisted of an opening, a middlegame, and an endgame, and a draw was not a valid outcome until all three phases had been wrung completely dry of possibilities. Agreeing to a draw merely because there was an equal position on the board was an act of disloyalty to the essential idea of a chess game.

Although Bobby's uncompromising attitude (which governed all aspects of his life) was natural to him and not a mask he wore to intimidate his opponents, it very definitely had that effect. Everyone who sat down to face him knew he was in for a struggle to the death. To his opponent the result of a game may have been relatively unimportant, but for Bobby it was *always* important.

And since Fischer had the creative imagination to discover winning chances in the most sterile positions and the technique to win with the most microscopic advantages, his refusal to compromise terrified many of his opponents. Psychologically, they were on the ropes even before the first blow was struck. This helps to explain the spectacular dimensions of some of his triumphs: winning a United States championship by a score of 11–0 (no draws), defeating such strong grandmasters as Taimanov and Larsen by match scores of 6–0 (no draws!), and, during his drive to the world championship, winning twenty straight games in top-level competition.

Bobby's ideals, taken at face value, are beyond dispute. He was right. Although for the rest of us such idealism is usually unattainable, I recommend adopting Fischer's attitude toward draws—i.e., playing every game to a finish—especially if you're still developing as a player. Agreeing to draws in the middlegame, equal or otherwise, deprives you of the opportunity to practice playing endgames, and the endgame is probably where you need the most practice. The best way to improve is to get a lot of experience under competitive conditions.

But since most of you are probably not geniuses of Fischer's caliber, and given the realities of tournament play, you should agree to draws under certain conditions.

TO DRAW OR NOT TO DRAW

The typical American open tournament is played in a single weekend, with two or three games a day. Even two games in a single day can be exhausting, and exhaustion increases in direct proportion to age.

Keeping that in mind, imagine that your first game of the day has reached an equal position and your opponent is about your own strength. In this case, maybe you should consider taking a draw.

In the first place, if your evaluation of the position is correct and it is truly equal, an unjustified winning attempt can cost you a full point. Second, if you try to win and the game is drawn anyway, your winning attempt would have cost you effort and energy you needed for the second game of the day. Third, if you know your opponent needs a win, your well-timed draw offer could provoke him to play too ambitiously and perhaps overreach himself and make a mistake.

Also, consider the playing schedule. If you play a long first game, you may not have time for a calm meal or a rest before the next game, and that could have dire consequences.

On the other hand, if your first opponent of the day is your rival for a top place in the tournament, some risk may be justified in trying to beat him, even in an equal position. Just remember not to get rattled if he offers you a draw!

Obviously, this book can't cover every situation that might arise in practice; there are too many variables. But when thinking about whether or not to offer or to accept a draw, you should consider not only the position on the board—that goes without saying—but also all the surrounding conditions, including, of course, the human element.

Many winning positions have been lost or drawn for reasons that had nothing to do with the position of the pieces, and many losses have been converted into draws or wins by the commonsense application of psychological factors. But it is useful to remember that most winning positions are, in fact, won on the board. Used intelligently, psychology is a valuable weapon, but it is not a substitute for knowledge, imagination, and technique.

The following games illustrate some of the psychological elements associated with draws.

BUDAPEST 1952
Slav Defense

M. Botvinnik	P. Benko
1 Nf3	Nf6
2 c4	c6

3 d4	d5
4 cxd5	cxd5

I seldom played the Slav Defense, and although I knew that Botvinnik had won a number of games with the Exchange Variation (4 cxd5), I entered it willingly because, frankly, I didn't think he could beat me in this symmetrical position. If I made no mistakes, he might get a slight edge in the endgame, but I was a good endgame player and was not worried about that possibility.

Naturally, I would have been delighted to draw against him with the black pieces. He was then the reigning world champion, after all, and I was just a twenty-four-year-old international master.

5 Nc3	Nc6
6 Bf4	e6
7 e3	Bd6
8 Bd3	

One of Botvinnik's successful innovations in this line. His idea is not to lose time retreating the bishop and to keep firm control of e5 in the event of 8 ... Bxf4, which would be fair compensation for the doubled f-pawns. 8 Bg3 is also playable. But 8 Bxd6 Qxd6 allows Black an early ... e5 with easy equality.

8 ...	Bxf4

8 ... Nxd4 is an interesting possibility, but after 9 Nxd4 e5 10 Bb5+ Black's king will have problems.

9 exf4	0-0
10 0-0	Bd7
11 Rc1	Na5

12 Ne5	Rc8
13 Qe2	

I was beginning to feel some pressure, so I decided to regroup and look for counterplay.

13 . . .	Nc6
14 Nf3	g6!?
15 Rfd1	Ne8
16 h4!	Nd6
17 g3	f6
18 Kg2	

Preparing h5 to break through on the kingside, but Botvinnik should have played 18 h5 at once. The text is a little slow.

18 . . .	Nf5
19 Bb1	h5!
20 Qd2	

With the strategic issues clouded, White might try for complications with 20 Bxf5 gxf5 21 Ne1 Qe8 22 Nb5.

20 . . .	Nce7
21 Re1	

Black's position in the center and on the kingside is impregnable, while White's d-pawn is a permanent weakness.

21 . . .	Qb6
22 b3	Qb4

Botvinnik, realizing that White's position offered little promise compared to Black's, offered me a draw.

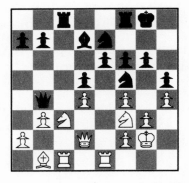

Although obviously I would have risked little by playing on, several psychological factors led me to accept.

This was the strongest tournament I had ever
played in. Also, this was my first game against a world
champion and my first against Botvinnik, a player I
greatly admired. For him to offer me a draw in one of
his pet variations was a considerable honor. I still get
a rush of pleasure when I remember the sound of his
voice saying, in German, "Wollen Sie Remis?"

Moreover, I had had a bad experience the day before against the Romanian international master
Troianescu. I had the foolish idea in those days that I
could beat anybody who wasn't a big-name grandmaster, and I would certainly not stoop to drawing
with a mere IM like Troianescu. Three times he offered me a draw, three times I declined, and finally I
lost.

I was not willing to tempt fate again so soon—and
certainly not against the world champion. Botvinnik
may have had to swallow his pride to offer me a
draw—but he, unlike me, had the wisdom to split the
point before it was too late.

As it turned out, in this tournament I ended up with
a better score against the big names than against the

"weakies." Later I understood why: My respect for the famous grandmasters prevented me from expecting too much.

DOES HE SEE WHAT I SEE?

Respect for your opponent is a healthy policy, but even that can be carried too far, as the following examples from Budapest 1952 illustrate.

P. Benko

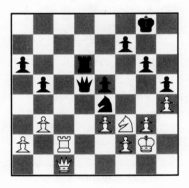

P. Keres

In this position, with White to move, I offered Keres a draw and he accepted. Black's threat of 31 . . . Rf6 is hard to meet, though 31 Qb2 might hold. I should at least have waited to see whether he would play that move before offering a draw. Simply put, I had so much respect for the legendary Estonian grandmaster that I turned chicken.

In my game against Harry Golombek the situation was reversed. Golombek, though much older and

more experienced than I, had never achieved a higher
rank than international master, whereas I was considered a promising young player and a sure bet to
become a grandmaster. Though I had the black pieces,
I was playing to win.

After seventeen moves we reached this position
with White to move:

P. Benko

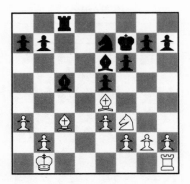

H. Golombek

I had just played 17 . . . Ne7. The two attacked black
pawns are taboo (18 Bxh7 g6 or 18 Bxb7 Rb8 followed
by . . . Bxa3), but as soon as I made my move I saw
that White could force a draw with 18 Bxe5 fxe5 19
Ng5+ Kf6 20 Nxh7+ Kf7 21 Ng5+, etc. So I offered
Golombek a draw, assuming he saw the same line.

Some players seem to lose their ability to view the
position objectively when offered a draw. I think that's
what happened to Golombek. We had reached an even
position, and he thought I was offering him a draw
because I realized that 17 . . . Ne7 was a mistake. That
part was true. What he didn't see was that the mistake

was allowing a forced draw; he thought he was getting the advantage and that I was afraid of him. Having thus deluded himself, he declined my draw offer
and played 18 Rc1.

Would he have played 18 Bxe5 if I hadn't offered
the draw? Maybe. Never ask yourself "what if" questions like that! They have no answers.

18 Rc1(?)	Bd6

No more draw. Now I started to think about winning again.

19 Bd2	Rxc1 +
20 Kxc1	b6
21 h3	h6
22 Bd3	g5
23 Kd1	Ng6
24 e4	h5
25 Be3	Bc5

Eliminating Black's bad bishop and White's good
one. The weakening of Black's queenside pawns is not
significant here.

26 Bxc5	bxc5
27 Kc2	Nf4
28 Bf1	Ke7
29 Ne1	Kd6
30 Kc3	Bd7
31 b3	h4
32 Nc2	g4
33 hxg4	Bxg4
34 f3?	

Overlooking Black's reply. 34 Ne3 is necessary.

34 ...   h3!

Winning a pawn. White must take the h-pawn, else
35 . . . h2, etc.

35 gxh3   Bxf3
36 Bd3   Nxh3

I eventually won a long endgame.

JUST SAY NO

If offering a draw can affect the opponent's judgment,
so can declining one. To wit:

P. Benko

R. Byrne

---

18 Rxd8

If memory serves, it was here that my opponent
offered me a draw. The position is quite even: There is
only one open file, the pawn structure is symmetrical,
neither side has any weaknesses, the bishops are of

opposite colors. Yet I had several good reasons for wanting to play on.

First, the tournament was a Swiss system open (in tournaments with very many players, it's impossible for everyone to play everyone else, so the Swiss pairing system is used to pair players with similar scores), and a draw with one of my rivals would do nothing to help me win first prize. Second, my chances of losing this endgame were nil, so I risked nothing by playing on.

Third—and the main reason I declined Byrne's draw offer—was the fact that I had beaten him several times and I knew I was an unpleasant opponent for him. The longer he had to sit facing me, the less he liked it.

18 . . .	Kxd8
19 Kd2	Kc7
20 Kc2	Nd7
21 g4	

White is worried about Black's threat to gain space with . . . f5 and . . . e4. Trying to impede that advance with e4 would create a serious weakness for White on d4. Now it will be hard for him to advance his e-pawn and f-pawn and they will become stationary targets. This isn't necessarily fatal, but it gives Black some initiative. In return, White will get the open g-file when Black plays . . . f5.

21 . . .	Nc5
22 Rd1	f5
23 gxf5	gxf5
24 Rg1	Ne6
25 e3	Bf6
26 Be2	Rf8
27 Rg2	

Black has some initiative, but there's nothing tangible yet. White defends his f-pawn in anticipation of Black's next move.

| 27 . . . | Bh4 |
| 28 Bh5 | Rf6 |

Black's initiative is growing. He now threatens to go after the h-pawn with . . . Rh6 and . . . Ng5.

Byrne was definitely unhappy. Not only was he being forced to play out a drawish position against an unpleasant opponent, he was also beginning to have problems holding the position. That probably explains the serious error he now commits, giving White control of several important squares.

29 e4?

White's well-known problem in the King's Indian Defense (the opening used in this game) is that, having played c4 and with Black's king bishop on the h8-a1 diagonal, White must not allow Black to get control of d4. Considering the caliber of my opponent, this mistake can be explained only by psychological factors.

| 29 . . . | f4! |
| 30 f3 | |

To prevent 30 . . . f3, which would have forced the disagreeable 31 Rh2. But what happens now is worse.

30 . . .	Rh6
31 Bg4	Nd4+
32 Kd1	Rg6

Threatening . . . h5, against which there is no satisfactory defense.

33 Rh2	h5
34 Bxh5	Rg1+
White resigned	

On 35 Kd2, Black can win the exchange with 35 . . . Bg3, or he can play for more with 35 . . . Rg5 and if 36 Bg4 Rxg4, etc.

ALL'S FAIR IN LOVE AND WAR— BUT NOT IN CHESS

Playing against Fischer some years ago, I offered him a draw in an equal position and he, of course, declined. Unable to squeeze anything out of the position, he finally started playing for little traps, trying to make me lose patience. At one point, I pretended to fall into his trap but at the last moment made the right move and gave him a look to let him know I understood what he was doing. The game was drawn in a few more moves.

Fischer was playing fair, as he always did. There is nothing wrong with trying to exploit the natural human tendency to become impatient when forced to play a boring position. But there are folks out there who will use unfair or unethical means to try to "steal" a draw or an advantage. Forewarned is forearmed.

The rules governing formal competition state that you may offer a draw only when your own clock is running and before you have made your move. Your opponent is not required to respond until after you have moved and stopped your clock. His response need not be verbal; for instance, he can decline your offer by simply making a move. You may not offer a draw again in the same game unless your opponent in the meantime has himself offered a draw.

The rule is supposed to prevent players from annoying their opponents by making repeated draw offers. If somebody is violating it deliberately to distract his opponents, he can be stopped by complaining to the tournament director.

But what can you do about somebody who stays technically within the rules by not making repeated verbal offers but who still tries to annoy you by staring, gesturing, or signaling?

Smile. Do not get upset. Complain to the director. And remember that the reason this guy is so eager to get a draw is that he doesn't like his position. The best way to teach him a lesson is to drag out the game, which will increase his anxiety. Stay cool, keep your eye on the ball, let *him* get upset.

One American master used to have another little trick. When he saw he was getting the worst of the game, especially against a lower-rated opponent, he would say to him, "Are you playing for a draw?" The innocent opponent, willing to draw, would get up from the table or in some other way accept the "offer." Later, finding a zero on the scoretable indicating that he had lost by time forfeit, he would go to the director to tell him it was a mistake, that the game was a draw.

But that tricky master, when asked to confirm his draw offer, would reply in wide-eyed innocence, "Who, me? I didn't offer him a draw. I only asked him if he was offering me one. Then he got up and left." The trick worked a couple of times, but later it was decided to interpret all such questions as binding draw offers.

That same American master would sometimes say to his opponent, "You played very well," and extend his hand—but without stopping his clock. His opponent, poor dope, would get up and leave, thinking the master had resigned. You can guess what happened when he saw a loss on the scoretable instead of a win. If you ever find yourself in a similar situation, make sure you aren't agreeing to something you don't want to agree to, and have your opponent stop his clock and sign the scoresheet.

There is no rule against offering a draw in a bad or even dead lost position, of course, and it isn't unethical either. But it only works if your opponent doesn't catch on fast enough.

I've never seen anyone do this better than the great Sammy Reshevsky, who was amazingly quick to realize when the tide was turning against him. Here's an example.

Mastichiadis

S. Reshevksy

This position occurred during the match between Greece and the United States at the 1950 Olympiad in Dubrovnik. Reshevsky had just played Nd2?, saw immediately that it was a blunder, and without hesitation offered Mastichiadis a draw. The Greek master, busy writing down Sammy's move, was so happy to get a draw with his illustrious opponent that he didn't even look at the position. If he had, he would have seen the winning move . . . Nxf2.

One more thing about draw offers: It sometimes happens that a player will seal a bad move when adjourning the game, and then offer a draw before play is resumed. If you smell a rat—or even if you don't—insist on seeing the sealed move before deciding whether or not to accept. Remember: Once he's made the draw offer, it remains on the table until you've either accepted or declined it.

The two golden rules about draw psychology:

1. Never offer a draw unless you're prepared for your opponent to accept it. Using draw offers to try to psych out your opponents is a dangerous game. If you offer a draw thinking your opponent is sure to turn it down, you could be in for a very unpleasant surprise.
2. Never accept a draw offer just because your opponent asks for one and you want him to like you. You know where nice guys finish. Look at the position: If you think it should be played out, play it out. If you think you can win, win.

■ ■ ■

CHAPTER 11

THE LAST ROUND AND OTHER CRISES

"There's No Tomorrow"
—Song title

At the critical point in some forgotten science fiction movie, when all seems lost, the hero explains to the heroine how he plans to defeat the entire enemy starfleet single-handedly. When the dubious young woman asks what will happen if the plan doesn't work, the hero replies, "They win."

In our humdrum daily lives we are seldom called upon to make decisions that will affect the lives of everyone in the universe for the next thousand years. But in sports and games, including chess, we do sometimes have to make absolute win-or-lose decisions under pressure. At such times, as in that science fiction movie, when losing is unthinkable, when it all comes down to a single crucial moment, when you must do it right this one time or it's all over and you've lost and the universe is doomed, that pressure can be quite considerable.

Crucial, do-or-die chess games typically occur in

the last round because that's the last chance to win a prize or to improve your rating or your score in the tournament. In open tournaments, where the Swiss system is employed to pair players with similar scores, it is in the final round that the tournament leaders can usually be found in a dramatic, all-or-nothing fight to the last pawn.

Some players, unable to endure the extraordinary tension of a bitter and often protracted fight, prefer to agree to a quick draw in the last round. But that lost half point can make all the difference, especially in an open tournament with relatively few rounds.

You can't win by resigning, says an old chess adage. And you can't win by agreeing to draws, either, says this not-so-old grandmaster.

If winning is important to you (why else would you be reading this book?), you may as well get used to the idea that in a no-compromise, kill-or-be-killed struggle you are going to feel some pressure. A *lot* of pressure. The question is: How can you deal with it so you don't blow your last chance?

First of all, make sure that a win is what you really need—no sense getting your nervous system all knotted up for nothing. Before the game, take a good look at your tournament standing and your opponent's. Maybe you can reach the score you want with a draw in your last game. Even better, maybe your opponent can reach his only by winning, in which case all the pressure will be on him.

If that's the situation you're in—your opponent needs to win but you don't—there are two things you should keep in mind.

1. In an all-or-nothing fight, a draw is the same as a loss. Expect your opponent to try everything—

sound, unsound, or desperate. This means you can never afford the luxury of relaxing.

2. See number 1.

If it's you who needs the win, naturally the pressure will be on you. But if you keep your mind on the game and your behind on the chair and don't allow yourself to be distracted, you'll be fine.

Of course, it's always possible that you will lose because your opponent is stronger than you. There's not much you can do about that sort of thing except get better. But if you must lose, don't let it be because you blew it under pressure or because you were distracted by the score.

A case in point was what happened to Gideon Stahlberg in his last-round game against me in the First Maroczy Memorial Tournament. Stahlberg, a Swedish grandmaster who died in 1962, was an adherent of the old-fashioned idea that Black's main task in the opening was to equalize. I knew he didn't like to take risks with the black pieces, and it was up to me to put that knowledge to practical use.

As the last round began, the standings were: Geller and Keres 11½, Stahlberg 11, Botvinnik and Smyslov 10, Pilnik and Szabo 9½, O'Kelly and Petrosian 8½, Barcza and Szily 8, Benko 7½, Golombek and Kottnauer 6½, Gereben 6, Troianescu 5, Sliwa 4½, Platz 2.

Keres was paired against Barcza, and Geller against O'Kelly. If Stahlberg beat me and if both Keres and Geller lost, he would win the tournament. If he lost and either Keres or Geller won, he could end up in third or fourth place. Obviously, this was a crucial game for him.

Although I was not in contention for a high place, this game was important to me too: winning it would give me the personal satisfaction of surpassing two of my countrymen in the tournament (Barcza and Szily).

Stahlberg's opening moves indicated that he would be satisfied with a draw. But I felt morally obligated to make a fight of it with White. The problem was how.

Stahlberg had a well-deserved reputation as a fine defensive player, so I couldn't afford to risk direct attack. Conversely, a slow, maneuvering struggle might not offer enough winning chances. I suspected that if Stahlberg saw a chance to play for a win, he might go for it despite his having the black pieces, considering his standing in the tournament. So I decided to entice him into a fight without risking too much myself. And I had to do it while we were still in the opening, before the outcomes of the Geller and Keres games could be predicted.

BUDAPEST 1952
Grünfeld Defense

P. Benko	G. Stahlberg
1 Nf3	d5
2 g3	Nf6
3 Bg2	g6
4 0-0	Bg7
5 d4	0-0
6 c4	c6

Playing it safe, since now 7 cxd5 cxd5 would give White only an insignificant edge in a symmetrical position.

7 Nbd2	Bf5
8 b3	Ne4
9 Bb2	a5
10 h3?!	

Threatening an eventual g4. This move, together with my next one, was a deliberate provocation. By offering my h-pawn in exchange for Black's d-pawn, I hoped that Stahlberg, with an eye toward winning the tournament, might try to exploit my weakened king position.

10 ...	Na6
11 Nh4	Be6?!(?)

It worked! Instead of playing the safe 11 ... Nxd2 12 Qxd2 Be6, Stahlberg falls victim to my psychological trap and allows himself to be tempted by the chance to expose my king. All he accomplishes, though, is to give me an open h-file.

12 Nxe4	dxe4
13 Bxe4	Bxh3
14 Bg2	Bxg2

Stahlberg decides to eliminate White's bishop to remove its strong influence from the center and to further weaken White's king. But forcing my king to g2 only makes it easier for me to get a rook to the h-file.

15 Kxg2	a4
16 Nf3	Qc7
17 Rh1	Rfd8
18 Qc1!	Nb8
19 d5!	

Black's king position will be weakened by the exchange of dark-square bishops, considering White's open h-file and the holes at f6 and h6. But the exchange is not to be avoided, for if 19 ... f6 20 Nd4 followed by Ne6. Of course, 19 . . . cxd5 20 Bxg7 Kxg7 can't be played because of 21 Qh6 + .

19 . . .	Bxb2
20 Qxb2	h5

Forced. This time 20 . . . cxd5 is met by 21 Rxh7!.

21 g4

Black's king position looks critical, but Stahlberg finds a defense.

21 . . .	cxd5
22 gxh5	Ra6!

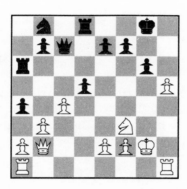

Just when I was congratulating myself on my cleverness and looking forward to a quick win, Stahlberg comes up with an unexpected resource, bringing his inactive queenside rook to the defense of his kingside.

Discouraged, I toyed with the idea of offering a draw. But when I pulled myself together and evaluated the position calmly, I saw that Stahlberg's good defensive move had merely granted him a temporary reprieve.

23 hxg6	Rxg6+
24 Kf1	d4?!

I was expecting Stahlberg to close the long diagonal this way. He was hoping for 25 Nxd4 Qe5 26 Rd1 Nc6 27 e3 Qe4 with a strong counterattack. But White has a much stronger way of going after the d-pawn, by avoiding the pin and still keeping up the threats on the kingside.

25 Qc2!	Qf4
26 Rh4	Qf6
27 Rd1	axb3
28 axb3	Nc6
29 Qe4	e5
30 b4	d3?!

Desperation, since 30 . . . Nxb4 31 Nxe5 Re8 32 Nd7! Qe7 33 Nf6+! wins for White, or if 30 . . . Re8 31 b5 Nd8, either 32 Nxd4 or 32 Rxd4 wins a pawn with the better position.

31 Rxd3	Ra8
32 Rd1	Qg7
33 b5	Nd4
34 Rh1	

Of course not 34 Qxe5 Rg1+. But now Black is lost. The game concluded: 34 . . . Nxf3 35 Qxf3 Re8 36 Qxb7 e4 37 Qd7 Qe5 38 Qh3 Qg7 39 c5 Rg5 40 Qe3 Kf8 41 b6. Black resigned after adjournment. The passed pawns win easily.

Meanwhile, Keres beat Barcza quickly, placing Geller under great pressure if he wanted to tie for first. But after seeing Keres's result, Geller gave O'Kelly a draw. Geller had been leading the tournament from the beginning, but, like a long-distance runner who suddenly runs out of breath, he couldn't keep up the pace all the way to the end. He only drew with his last four opponents, though all were weaker players.

In big open tournaments, the pressure can be even greater because of the large cash prizes that are at stake, and also because of the magnified importance of every half point in a short tournament.

Take the 1986 New York Open, for instance, where I was in contention for first prize. My last-round opponent was Hungarian Grandmaster Gyula Sax. If I won I would earn $12,000, but if I drew I would get only $3,000. Sax offered me a draw at a point when I had some advantage, though it would have been difficult to exploit. I turned him down, blundered in time pressure, and lost. So instead of winning $12,000 or $3,000, I got nothing.

Refusing Sax's draw offer was a costly decision, but I don't regret it. Similar gambles have paid off for me many times. What I regret is the ten valuable minutes I spent thinking about his offer, ten minutes that would have come in very handy indeed later on.

■ ■ ■

CHAPTER 12

THE TROUBLE WITH WOMEN (AND COMPUTERS)

Why can't a woman be more like a man?
—Prof. Henry Higgins, *My Fair Lady*

"I consider it unworthy and degrading to lose against a female. Women can never be as good as men in chess. They can get a certain degree of theoretical knowledge, but in a game of brain versus brain, where you can't follow theory, they are without a chance."

So said Swedish grandmaster Ulf Andersson in the newspaper *Svenska Dagbladet.* Since Andersson's views on the capabilities of the human female have no more validity than those of anyone else who is not a trained psychologist or sociologist, what we see here is a display of raw male ego. We have seen it before, in similar words spoken by other grandmasters:

Bobby Fischer, interviewed in *Harper's* magazine, January 1962: "They're all weak, all women. They're stupid compared to men. They shouldn't play chess, you know. They're like beginners. They lose every single game against a man. There isn't a woman player in the world I can't give knight odds to and still beat."

Gary Kasparov, interviewed in *Playboy* magazine, November 1989: "Chess does not fit women properly. It's a fight, you know? A big fight. It's not for women. . . . Chess is the combination of sport, art and science. In all these fields, you can see men's superiority. . . . Probably the answer is in the genes."

Although in earlier times even the best women players were relatively weak, that is no longer the case. Such women as world champions Nona Gaprindashvili and Maya Chiburdanidze, and more recently the Polgar sisters, have proved that the supposed "natural" inferiority of women in chess is a myth. If men feel it is "unworthy and degrading" to lose to a woman, they have only themselves to blame for having created the delusion that women are "naturally" inferior.

Nevertheless, it is undeniable that men have always far outnumbered women in chess, and probably always will. So the question is not "Why can't women play chess?" but rather "Why *don't* they?"

Nobody really knows. But everybody has a theory.

Some psychiatrists think it's Oedipal: chess, they say, is symbolic father-murder (checkmate) with a strong attachment to the mother (the queen), which is why the game appeals to boys more than it does to girls.

Some sociologists say it's the result of children having been taught through the ages that war and aggression (including, by implication, chess) were for the menfolk: little boys played with toy soldiers and learned how to do war; little girls played with dolls and prepared for motherhood.

Some biologists have said it's genetic: boys don't have to be taught to want to fight, or girls to want to be mothers; they have been thus programmed by nature.

Much as the chess world would like to see this matter settled once and for all, that's beyond the purpose of this book. What is of concern here is the acute discomfort that many men feel when they are sitting across a chessboard from a woman.

In chess as in most forms of competition, men generally consider that they are superior to women and that the natural outcome of a contest of skill between the sexes is a win by the stronger side; i.e., the male. The trouble is, there is a very real possibility that he will lose. His fear of that "unworthy and degrading" outcome turns up the psychological heat, which increases the likelihood that he will blunder—a vicious circle.

The first recognized woman master, in fact the first women's world champion, was the Czech-born Englishwoman Vera Menchik, who played in the 1920s and '30s (she was killed in the bombing of London during World War II).

Though her strength was probably that of international master (i.e., just below grandmaster), she defeated a surprising number of much higher-ranking male players. Those who lost to her earned membership in the "Vera Club," an unofficial and semi-humorous recognition not of her successes but of her victims' unaccountable failure to beat her.

The existence of the Vera Club pretty well defined the prevailing male attitude toward women players in those days (an attitude that still prevails, unfortunately): A man who had the misfortune to lose to a woman became an object of ridicule—gentle ridicule, to be sure, but ridicule nonetheless.

Objective analysis of Menchik's wins against grandmasters proves that in most cases the losers made obvious blunders and played far below their level. It can fairly be said that they lost rather than that

Menchik won. Clearly they were afflicted by the extra psychological pressure of competing against a woman—which is understandable considering the almost complete absence of women players at that level in those days.

Here's an example of the Menchik phenomenon.

HASTINGS 1930–31

V. Menchik

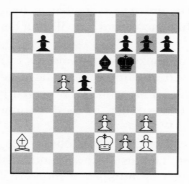

M. Euwe

Euwe was then one of the world's leading grandmasters and would in a few years become world champion by defeating the mighty Alekhine. He appears to have a slightly superior position here thanks to his better bishop and his pressure on Black's d-pawn. But because of his doubled g-pawns, he does not have enough to win.

38 Kd3	Ke5
39 g4!?	

If 39 f4+ Kf5 40 Kd4 Kg4! 41 Bxd5 Bxd5 42 Kxd5 Kxg3 43 Kd6 Kxg2 44 Kc7 h5, etc., and the game is a draw because both players will get new queens.

39 ...	g5!
40 g3	Bxg4
41 f4+	gxf4
42 gxf4+	Kf6

If 42 ... Ke6? 43 e4!

43 Bxd5	Bc8

White's doubled pawns have disappeared, but now Black's h-pawn threatens to come alive.

44 Bf3	Ke7
45 Kd4	Kd8
46 Kd5	b6!

Thus Black rids herself of her weak b-pawn, since if 47 cxb6 Bb7+ wins.

47 c6

Here and later, White refuses to acknowledge that the game is a draw, which would be obvious after, for instance, 47 Kc6 bxc5 48 Kxc5. Instead, he allows Black to have two passed pawns.

47 ...	Kc7
48 Ke5	Be6
49 f5	Bb3
50 Kf6	b5
51 Kg7	b4
52 Kxh7	Bc2
53 Kg7	

Euwe still insists on playing for a win, unable to accept the fact that the best he can hope for is a draw after 53 Bd5.

53 . . .	b3
54 Bd5	b2
55 Ba2	Kxc6
56 f6	Kd6
57 e4	Bxe4
58 Kxf7	Bd5 +
59 Bxd5	b1(Q)
60 Kg7	Qg1 +
61 Kf8	Kxd5

White resigned

I too have had uncomfortable experiences playing against women. In Lone Pine 1975, for instance, Alla Kushnir, then the second-best woman player in the world (she had played and lost two matches for the women's world championship), started the tournament by beating Grandmaster Larry Evans. That caused a sensation of sufficient magnitude that Bobby Fischer called me up to ask how Evans explained the fiasco!

In the second round it was my turn to play Kushnir. Before the game I had to endure some teasing by my male colleagues, and during play I was very nervous, twice allowing Kushnir to escape from bad positions. At adjournment I had only a slight edge and wasn't at all sure it would be enough to win. Thanks to my better adjournment analysis, I finally got the full point when she missed the best continuation.

Kushnir ended up occupying a high place in the tournament scoretable, having added a few grand-master scalps to her already impressive collection.

A later Lone Pine tournament boasted the participation of Nona Gaprindashvili, then the women's world champion. Although she finished in a four-way tie for first place, her impressive score was not a true reflection of the quality of her games: her opponents played as though hypnotized.

I remember studying the scoretable with a worried Grandmaster Anatoly Lein after several rounds had been played. "If we go on like this," he moaned, "we're in danger of playing Nona."

Lein finally did have to play her, and although he obtained much the better game, he was so nervous that he eventually lost. Like so many other men who have faced her across the board, he could not handle the psychological pressure.

Adults suffer similar psychological discomfort in competition against children, and for a similar reason: The "natural" result would be a win for the more experienced and knowledgeable adult; a loss would be "unworthy and degrading."

My father taught me to play chess when I was a child, and as soon as I was able to beat him he no longer wanted to play with me. This is not hard to understand. Losing to a child is a blow to the adult ego; when the child is your own, the conflicting emotions make the blow much more damaging.

In his fine book *Searching for Bobby Fischer*, Fred Waitzkin describes his emotions as he and his son, Josh, a seven-year-old chess prodigy, exchanged roles:

> While I tried to slaughter Josh, I rooted for him to win. The game became a quicksand of passion for us. After an emotional loss, he would pretend not to care, but his lower lip would tremble. Dejected, he'd go off to his room and my heart would be broken. My carefully crafted victories felt like defeats. . . .
>
> Excited as I was by his burgeoning and inexplicable

■ ■ ■ ■ ■

chess talent, I found it unsettling that he could calculate
exchanges more accurately and three times faster than I
could. He beat me game after game. Losing to him made
me feel old and dull. There were times when . . . I'd want
to wrestle him to the ground and pin his arms.

My early successes against my father, though bad
for his ego, were good for mine, and they inspired me
to study chess more seriously. But as I grew to man-
hood I began to understand how he must have felt. I
received my first taste of that psychological discomfort
when I met the fifteen-year-old Bobby Fischer,
the greatest chess prodigy of his generation. More recently, at the 1988 New York Open, I was paired
with the greatest chess prodigy of this generation,
Judit Polgar.

Judit is not only a child—she was twelve years old
when the following game was played—but also a girl.
Complicating matters still further was that Judit and
her older sisters, Zsuzsa and Sofia, are my chess stu-
dents in Hungary. All things considered, not the least
of which is the fact that Judit is a very strong player,
I would have preferred to skip the ordeal of playing
against her.

NEW YORK 1988
Sicilian Defense

J. Polgar	P. Benko
1 e4	c5
2 Nf3	d6
3 d4	cxd4
4 Nxd4	Nf6
5 Nc3	Nc6
6 Bc4	Qb6

As on other occasions, I chose a move of my own invention that was unknown to my opponent.

7 Nb3	e6
8 Be3	Qc7
9 0-0	a6
10 a4	b6
11 f3	Be7
12 Qe1	0-0
13 Qf2	

With 11 f3, White chose a cautious setup that should not give Black any particular difficulty. Up to this point I had used only five minutes on the clock, but now I thought for about twenty minutes.

Obviously, my b-pawn is under attack. The natural move is 13 ... Rb8, and after 14 Rfd1 Nb4 15 Bf1 d5 Black has the initiative and a promising game. Indeed, that's exactly how my opponent intended to play, as she told me later. I wanted to improve that variation by forcing White's bishop to d3, where I could trade it off at my convenience, but my move was a serious blunder.

Mistakes of such seriousness this early in the game

are rare in master play. If I were superstitious, I could blame it on the number thirteen. Since I'm not, I can only suggest that it was caused by abnormal psychological pressure. I don't believe I would have made such a mistake against an adult male opponent.

13 . . .	Nb4??
14 Bxb6!	

A bolt from Budapest! Judit told me that she discovered this little combination while I was pondering my previous move. If 14 . . . Qxc4 15 Na5 and there is no safe place for the black queen.

14 . . .	Qb8
15 a5	Bd7

Black is lost, since he has a cramped position and no compensation for the lost pawn. Once I got over my shock, I decided that since I had nothing to lose I would try to make a real fight of it.

16 Rfd1	Rc8
17 Bf1	Be8
18 Rd2	d5
19 Re1	dxe4
20 Nxe4	Nfd5

Having freed my position somewhat and developed a couple of threats, I offered a "tactical" draw here, which my opponent confidently refused.

21 c4	Nxb6
22 axb6	Bc6(?)

The immediate 22 . . . a5 is better.

23 Kh1?

Too cautious. After the game Judit told me she had originally planned 23 Na5 Bxe4 24 Rxe4 (the exchange sacrifice *24 fxe4! Bc5 25 Rd8 + ! Rxd8 26 Qxc5* is strong) 24 . . . f5 25 Rxe6 Bc5 26 Re8 + , but rejected it because of 26 . . . Kf7.

23 . . .	a5
24 Nc3	a4
25 Nc1	Be8
26 Ne4	f5
27 Ng3	Bc5
28 Qe2	Bf7
29 Rd7	Qxb6

Black has won back the pawn and has a superior position. Now it was Judit's turn to offer a draw, but I decided to play on to punish her for refusing my earlier offer.

30 Qe5	Nc6
31 Qe2	Nd4
32 Qe5	Nc6
33 Qe2	Rc7
34 Rxc7	Qxc7

35 Nd3	Bd4
36 Qc2	Ra5
37 f4	g6
38 Ne2	Bf6
39 b4	axb3
40 Qxb3	e5
41 fxe5	Nxe5
42 Nxe5	Bxe5
43 Nc3?!	

White tries to be active, since 43 Ng3 Rc5 44 Rc1 h5 45 Bd3 h4 46 Nf1 h3 is quite strong for Black.

43 . . .	Qc5?!

After 43 . . . Bxh2 44 Nd5 Bxd5 45 cxd5 Bd6 White has winning chances despite the opposite-color bishops because of White's exposed king.

44 Nd5	Qf2
45 Qe3	Qxe3
46 Nxe3	Kg7
47 g3	Ra1

This was, in effect, a draw offer. Our game, the second round of the day, had started in the early evening and it was now midnight. The many spectators gathered around our table were making me rather uncomfortable, since I had the feeling they thought I was a monster for torturing the little girl instead of letting her go to sleep.

48 Rxa1	Bxa1
49 Kg2	Kf6
50 Kf3	Bd4
51 Nd5+	Ke5
52 g4	Be6

And here we finally agreed to a draw.

Judit followed this tournament with results that surpassed even those of Fischer and Kasparov at the same age. Many experts predict that this young woman will open a new chapter in the history of chess by being the first female to challenge, and perhaps defeat, the male world champion.

There is no doubt that the strength and the number of women players have increased dramatically in recent years. Inevitably, the typically scornful male attitude must give way to respect. And the sooner the better, since men's condescension toward women is responsible for the psychological pressure they feel when competing against them.

HOW CAN YOU PSYCH OUT A CHESS COMPUTER?

Computers are everywhere, including chess tournaments. If you haven't already played against one, you will, sooner or later. Of course you will want to beat the thing to uphold the honor of the human race. But how do you beat a machine that sees everything, calculates with perfect accuracy, never gets into time trouble, and doesn't know or care who its opponent is?

"If a human player was beaten as decisively as I just beat Deep Thought," said World Champion Gary Kasparov after winning his first game against the world's strongest computer chess program, "he would be so intimidated that he would be an easy target in the next game. But not a machine. It cannot be intimidated."

Playing against computers makes many people uncomfortable. But it shouldn't. Think of it as a scientific experiment, and consider yourself fortunate to be living in an age of miracles in which you can have such a marvelous opportunity.

If you own a chess computer, you already know a few things about it. You know, for instance, that it can't be distracted, does not become mentally or physically fatigued, and never gets discouraged—in sum, it is impervious to all the psychological ploys described in this book.

But we humans are *not* impervious, so we must be on our guard lest that mass of wires and silicon get the better of us simply because we allow ourselves to be intimidated by it.

When it comes to calculating variations, we poor humans can't match the computer's ability to analyze millions of moves in a few seconds. But even the best computers are relatively weak in strategy, and that's where we have the advantage. So to improve your results against computers, avoid tactical skirmishes and steer instead for the type of game in which the better long-range plan will carry the day.

Because computers calculate with relentless accuracy, it's important to avoid tactical errors. The only game I ever lost to a computer was in a simultaneous exhibition against ten computers in Australia. One careless slip on my part was enough: after that everything was forced, and soon the computer lit up like a Christmas tree and announced mate in five.

If you get safely through the middlegame with an equal or even slightly inferior position, you still have a good chance of winning, because the endgame is where the computer is at its worst.

The strategic principles that apply to the middlegame are quite different from those of the endgame. For example, in the middlegame the king usually must be protected far from the main battle, but in the endgame the king often becomes the chief protagonist. So far, programmers have not found a way to make a computer reconcile these conflicting strategic principles in a single game.

For example, look at the following conclusion of a game between the world's strongest chess program and the former human world champion. It was played at Harvard University in 1990.

Deep Thought

Anatoly Karpov

The computer has played the opening and middle-game quite well and even has an extra pawn. Here it could take an easy draw with 45 ... h6+ 46 Kxh6 Rh4+ 47 Kg5 Rh5+ 48 Kf4 Rf5+ and ... Rxe5. But having no respect for its illustrious opponent and overestimating the value of its extra pawn, it plays for a win.

45 ...	a4
46 f4	h6 +

White would be forced to take a draw after 46 . . . Rd2, but the text is still OK.

47 Kg4	Rc4

The computer had plenty of time, which it should have used to consider drawing with 47 . . . g5 or 47 . . . Rd2.

48 h4	Rd4??

Black's last two moves merely wasted time and allowed White to improve his position. Only 48 . . . d4 or 48 . . . Rc1 make sense.

49 Rf6 +	Kg7
50 Ra6	Kf7
51 h5!	gxh5 + ?

Even now, 51 . . . g5 still offers chances to draw. The computer seems not to understand that what matters in the endgame is not how many pawns you have but how good they are.

52 Kf5!

It's hard to believe that such a strong computer could have seen this move and done nothing to prevent it. White's connected passed pawns are not only potent in themselves but also create mating threats.

The rest was a breeze for Karpov: 52 . . . Kg7 53 Ra7+ Kf8 54 e6 Re4(?) (54 . . . h4?! is a better try) 55 Rd7 Rc4 56 Rxd5 h4 57 Rd3 Ke7 58 Rd7+ Kf8 59 Rh7 h5 60 Ke5 h3 61 f5 Kg8 62 Rxh5 a3 63 Rxh3 a2 64 Ra3 Rc5+ 65 Kf6 and the computer resigned.

■ ■ ■ ■ ■

One last word about playing computers: They are getting stronger every day, and despite your best efforts, sooner or later they will beat you (if they aren't doing it now). Don't take it too hard—you're in good company. Computers have already beaten Bent Larsen, Tony Miles, Robert Byrne, and other high-ranking grandmasters, and it won't be too long before the world champion's name is added to the list.

■

CHAPTER 13

ATTACK, DEFENSE, AND COUNTERATTACK

If you wanted to compile an anthology of chess games and hoped to sell a lot of copies of it, you would be wise to fill it with attacking games abounding in daredevil sacrifices and dazzling combinations. Those are the games that chess lovers delight in, and the players who ignite that kind of fireworks on the chessboard—players like Morphy, Alekhine, Tal, Keres, and Kasparov—are the most acclaimed superstars of the chess arena.

But for every game won through brilliant attack, another is won and countless others drawn through brilliant defense. Nevertheless, most people do not highly esteem even the greatest defensive players—such as Steinitz, Petrosian, and Karpov, to mention only the world champions—whose genius lies not in creating brilliant attacks but in preventing them. Such players are less appreciated because their successes are not obvious, like checkmate, but are hidden beneath the surface to be revealed only by probing analysis. Masters of the defense are often—and quite unfairly—denigrated as boring technicians.

Naturally, everyone dreams of playing like Tal—creating immortal combinations and seeing their games published in newspapers and magazines all over the world with an exclamation mark dangling from every other move. But Tal is an extraordinary genius. For the rest of us, it's important to be realistic about the position on the board so that we aren't tempted to launch an attack when there are no grounds for attack.

Nona Gaprindashvili, for many years the women's world champion, was once asked after a disastrous result how she could have allowed it to happen. "I have been told," she replied, "that I play like Tal in a skirt, so I tried to mate all my opponents."

Unfortunately, you can't create a mating attack out of pure desire; the possibility must be inherent in the position, and not every position justifies an attacking strategy. Sometimes you have to maneuver patiently and wait for your chance—which may never come. Sometimes you have to defend.

It's very easy in the heat of battle to overestimate your resources or the strength of your attack, or to overlook the resources of the defense, or to underestimate the determination of the defender. If aggressive attack is your cup of tea, *calculate accurately*. It is not a good feeling to sacrifice a piece and a few moves later find out that your opponent has a saving defensive shot that leaves you a piece down with no attack.

Analyze, don't guess. The so-called intuitive (i.e., uncalculated) sacrifice usually turns out to be a mistake because of an unforeseen defense. After you've lost, it is no consolation to say, "I didn't see it."

In my game with Bobby Fischer in his last United

States Championship (1966–67), we reached this complicated position after twenty-three moves.

R. Fischer

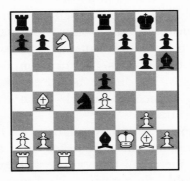

P. Benko

Bobby's last move was 23 . . . Bh6, and I replied 24 Re1?. After some further complications, I got the worst of it and finally lost.

Why didn't I take one of his rooks? Because I didn't analyze far enough. I saw 24 Nxa8! Bxc1 25 Nc7! Bxb2 26 Rb1 Rc8 27 Nd5! Rc2, and didn't like my position. Had I looked one move further, I would have seen the winning move 28 Ne3!.

And why did Fischer offer to sacrifice the exchange if three moves later he would get a lost position? For the same reason: he didn't analyze far enough. Even when I told him the next day that I could have won after 24 Nxa8, he refused to believe it until I showed him 28 Ne3.

THE DEFENSE NEVER RESTS

It is not wimpy to defend yourself. Being on the defensive does not mean you're losing. In fact, if your opponent has sacrificed material to get the attack, you will end up with a material advantage and possibly a won game if you defend successfully.

Of course, you have to know when not to accept a sacrifice. Often the clock plays a crucial role. In my last game against Tal, in Hastings 1973, I sensed that his piece sacrifice was unsound (it was, as analysis proved later), but with no time to find the refutation, I decided not to accept it. That meant continuing the game a pawn down, but I was counting on Tal's relatively poor endgame technique. Indeed, at the end it was he who was a pawn down and begging for a draw.

In Caracas 1970, Karpov found one good defense after another against my attacks. Worried about my approaching time pressure, I offered him a draw in a still somewhat better position, and he accepted. Fischer said later that he would never have given him a draw in that position and showed me how he would have won. His analysis was right—but he wasn't the one in time pressure against Karpov.

When you defend, try not to worry or become upset. Keep cool and trust your position—it's all you've got. Even if it's bad, sell your life as dearly as possible. Put up as many obstacles as you can to make things difficult for the attacker. It very often happens that he will overreach himself, or get impatient or discouraged, or become tired and lose his way in the complications.

Tal is known for the completely unexpected sacrifices he likes to throw at his opponents, especially when they're in time pressure. Later analysis often proves those sacrifices to be unsound, but they aren't meant to be 100 percent correct—their purpose is to induce psychological shock.

"I recall how in some of my games with Smyslov," Tal said in a lecture in the Soviet Union, "when it seemed I was completely lost, I was desperate and had no choice but to launch knowingly incorrect tactical maneuvers. . . . Now this has become merely a psychological device with which many chess players arm themselves."

It's White's move in the following position from a Soviet championship. He seems about to lose his e-pawn without compensation, so he does what he can to confuse the issue.

V. Smyslov

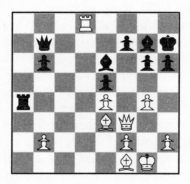

A. Gipslis

Gipslis made a desperate bid for complications with 34 Bxh6?!. Now 34 . . . Bxh6 is no good because of 35 Qf6 Bg7 36 Qh4+ Bh6 37 g5 and White wins. But Black can accept the sacrifice with 34 . . . Kxh6 35 Qh3+ Kg5, though his wandering king will need protection for a while.

Instead, Smyslov played 34 . . . Qxe4, giving up his winning chances. Tal, who was watching the game, said later he knew Smyslov would not take the bishop "because he does not trust himself in calculating con-

crete variations." After the game, Smyslov told Tal he was worried about the possible dangers if he took the bishop.

It's a wise player who recognizes danger and does something about it, although in this case Smyslov was probably too cautious. What's not so wise is to try to do something about danger that isn't really there, which brings us to a famous adage attributed to the great player and theoretician Aron Nimzovich: "The threat is stronger than the execution."

IS THE THREAT REALLY STRONGER THAN THE EXECUTION?

Lives there a chess player who has never heard that adage? Like an advertising slogan, it's been printed in so many books and magazine articles that we've come to accept it without questioning its accuracy.

In fact it isn't entirely accurate. But it does say something important, and because it has particular relevance to chess psychology it deserves to be examined more closely.

What the adage means, generally, is this: When your threat forces your opponent to do something he may not have wanted to do, then the threat has served a purpose even though it may not be carried out. This is of course one of the fundamentals of chess strategy and tactics.

But common sense tells you that making a threat should not be more effective than carrying it out, though that's what the adage literally says. If you threaten mate and your opponent gives up a pawn to stop it, the threat has won a pawn, but checkmate would obviously have been stronger.

But suppose your opponent, thinking your threat is stronger than it really is, takes unnecessarily drastic preventive measures, like sacrificing material or wrecking his pawn structure. Only then is the threat truly stronger than its execution. This is one of the fundamentals of chess psychology.

Look at this position, from a game I witnessed at the Women's International, Rio de Janeiro 1979, with White to make her 33d move.

Milunka Lazarevic

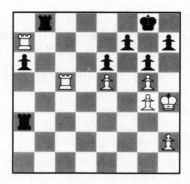

Rachel Crotto

Crotto saw Black's coming 33 . . . Rbb3 followed by mate at h3, thought there wasn't a blessed thing she could do about it, and so she resigned.

That was a mistake. Discouraged by the apparently unstoppable threat of mate, Crotto did not look deeply enough into the position. Had she done so, she might have found the saving resource I showed her after the game: 33 h3!.

Now if 33 . . . Rbb3 34 Rc8+ Kg7 35 Rg8+! Kxg8 36 Ra8+ Kg7 37 Rg8+ Kxg8 stalemate (the point of 33 h3). If Black tries to avoid that line by advancing a kingside pawn, White's king is freed from its prison.

Black, with an extra pawn, might have won anyway after 33 h3, though neither Lazarevic nor anyone else at the tournament was able to demonstrate a win. As Crotto saw too late, Lazarevic's threat was stronger than its execution.

THE PSYCHOLOGICAL POWER
OF HITTING BACK

The kind of game that gives me the most pleasure, whether I'm one of the players or following the score at home, is one in which a strong attack has been withstood and the defender gets his revenge with a powerful counterattack.

The daredevil counterattacker of our time is unquestionably Viktor Korchnoi. He loves to provoke his opponents into attacking him, usually by making seemingly careless moves. Like all counterattackers, Korchnoi is a great defender. If he weren't, he'd never get a chance to counterattack. I was amazed at the kind of attack he was willing to endure against me at Stockholm 1961, and further amazed that he survived.

Korchnoi is also a savvy psychologist in the Lasker mold, and knows that a counterattack can often be more effective than the attack that preceded it. The attacker, his resources exhausted, his attack over, his pieces misplaced for defense, is at a low ebb psychologically and ripe for the taking.

If you like to counterattack, the Indian defenses and the Sicilian Defense are the openings you should be studying for Black. Though they're called defenses, the King's Indian, Nimzo-Indian, and more recently even the once-stodgy Queen's Indian are excellent choices for the counterattacker because in most variations they allow Black's pieces free development, though sometimes at the cost of pawn weaknesses.

The Sicilian Defense, one of the most popular responses to 1 e4, is another opening in that category. Here's an example.

HUNGARIAN CHAMPIONSHIP 1951
Sicilian Defense

L. Szabo	P. Benko
1 e4	c5

As innumerable manuals have pointed out, White's first move stakes a claim to several center squares while Black's, rather than disputing that claim, looks toward controlling a different area of the board. Already the dim contours of counterattack can be perceived in the far distance.

2 Nf3	Nc6
3 d4	cxd4
4 Nxd4	Nf6
5 Nc3	d6
6 Bc4	

This bishop move, already in vogue when Bobby Fischer was just learning the game, was later to become one of his pet variations against the Sicilian.

6 ...	e6
7 0-0	Be7
8 Be3	0-0
9 Bb3	Bd7
10 f4	Nxd4
11 Bxd4	Bc6
12 Qd3	

Better is 12 Qe2, but the line Black is playing was an invention of mine that was then an unfamiliar novelty. About five years later, when Soviet Grandmaster Yefim Geller started playing it, the Russians dubbed it the Geller Variation.

I once got into a friendly argument with Grandmaster Yuri Averbakh about Boleslavsky's book on the Sicilian Defense, which had just been published. Looking in the index, I could find no mention of the Najdorf Variation. I asked Averbakh how could a book on the Sicilian not include the Najdorf Variation. He insisted the Najdorf was in the book, and finally we made a bet.

I got the book, handed it to him, and asked him to show me the Najdorf Variation. "Here it is," he said, showing me the familiar series of moves. But the variation, instead of bearing Najdorf's name, bore no name at all.

Which reminds me of a joke they like to tell in Hungary. At a technology exhibition in Moscow, every great invention, from the telephone to the internal combustion engine, is identified as "Invented by Ivan Ivanovich Ivanov." Near the exit is a large portrait. "Is that Ivan Ivanovich Ivanov, the man who invented all these things?" asks a visitor. "No," replies his friend. "That's the man who invented Ivan Ivanovich Ivanov."

12 . . .	b5
13 Nxb5	Bxe4
14 Qe2	Qd7
15 c4	d5?!
16 Rad1	Qb7
17 cxd5	Bxd5
18 Bxd5	Nxd5
19 f5!	a6
20 Nc3	Nxc3
21 bxc3	exf5
22 Rxf5	

With 15 . . . d5?!, Black opened the center too early. I should have played 15 . . . Bc6. Now White is better developed and has a strong bishop, which Black should think about neutralizing with . . . f6.

22 . . .	Rad8?!
23 Re1	Bd6?!

More prudent is 23 . . . Rd7, but not 23 . . . Rfe8 because of the pin 24 Re5.

24 Qg4	g6

This looks awful, but Black can't play 24 . . . f6 now because of 25 Rxf6.

25 Qg5

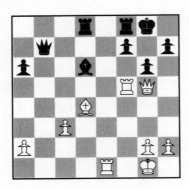

White's attack is in full swing. Despite such dire threats as Qf6, I tried to keep calm.

25 . . .   Bb8!?

A strange-looking defensive move, but actually the best under the circumstances, preparing either . . .

Rxd4 or . . . Ba7 to get rid of White's strong bishop.
For instance: 26 Qf6 Rxd4 27 cxd4 gxf5 and White has
to be satisfied with perpetual check.

If 26 Re7!? Qb1+ 27 Rf1 Bxh2+. With time pressure approaching, it isn't surprising that White elects
to preserve his bishop rather than enter that complicated continuation.

| 26 Bf6 | Rd6 |

Still hanging in there. If now 27 Qh6 Qb6+ 28 Bd4
Rxd4 29 cxd4 Qxd4+ 30 Rf2 Ba7, Black not only wins
back the exchange but comes out a pawn up. Or if 27
Be7 Re8.

| 27 Kh1 | Re6 |
| 28 Ref1 | |

It appears that Black has no defense against Qh6
and that White has finally reached his goal. If 28 . . .
Re2 29 R5f3 wins.

But in fact White's attack is over. Now comes the
unexpected counterattack.

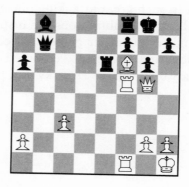

| 28 . . . | Qc7! |
| 29 g3 | |

There is nothing better. If 29 Qh6 Qxh2 + !, or 29 R5f4 Qxf4 wins.

29 . . .   Qc6 +
30 R5f3

White, still involved in his own attack, does not realize the strength of Black's counterattack. Better is 30 R1f3, though 30 . . . Be5 then kills the f6 bishop, after which White may not even be able to get a draw. After the text move, the end comes faster.

30 . . .   Re1!

With the double threat of 31 . . . Qxf3 + and 31 . . . Rxf1 + . Now everything is forced, since 31 Kg1 Qxf3 transposes to the game.

31 Rxe1   Qxf3 +
32 Kg1   Ba7 +
33 Bd4   Qxc3!
        White resigned

According to such great attacking players as Bronstein and Tal, most combinations are inspired by the player's memories of earlier games. My combination against Szabo, for instance, reminded me of an endgame study by the great Troitzky that I had solved years earlier.

A. A. Troitzky, 1927

White to play and win

The solution is 1 c6 b2 2 c7 b1(Q) 3 c8(Q)+ Ka7 4 Qc7+ Ka8 5 Bg2+ Be4 6 Qh7!! Kb8 7 Bxe4 wins.

I always urge players to study composed problems and endgames. The themes and patterns their creators demonstrate, often in beautiful and memorable ways, arise in practical games more often than you might think.

■■■■■
CHAPTER 14

TO ERR IS HUMAN; TO FORGIVE, FOOLHARDY

A blunder is a special type of mistake. It should not be confused with an inaccuracy, which is a minor slip that may not be particularly damaging, or with an error in strategy or positional judgment. A blunder is a bungle, a boner, a bobble, a boo-boo. Its effects are more or less immediate and obvious, such as losing a piece. It is usually the result of inadvertence or oversight or faulty calculation.

We all blunder occasionally—some of us more occasionally than others—and usually for the same reasons. We are tired or distracted or in time pressure or discouraged or unprepared for a sudden change in the position. Being human, you might as well get used to the idea that you have not yet made your last blunder.

But a blunder is not the end of the world. It only hurts if your opponent recognizes it for what it is and exploits it correctly—which is by no means a sure thing.

One of the causes of blundering is, as we noted above, failure to adjust to a new situation. When you blunder, you throw the game suddenly in an unexpected direction. Your opponent, intent on his own plans, may not even realize that you've made a mistake. Or, thinking that you're setting a trap, he may waste valuable time working it out. Or maybe he'll get so excited that he will blunder in return.

Often, a player who receives the gift of an opponent's blunder thinks he has already won the game and gets careless. For example, here's a game from my first international tournament, with White to move.

BAD GASTEIN 1948

Galia

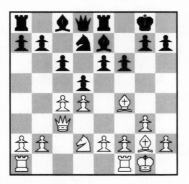

P. Benko

My opponent's 11 . . . f6 was an odd-looking move that should have put me on my guard. After his last move, 12 . . . Re8, I saw the trap 13 cxd5 exd5 14 Bxd5 + ? cxd5 15 Bc7 Bb4! and Black comes out a piece ahead. Thinking that Black was simply prepar-

ing the reasonable . . . Nf8, I unsuspectingly continued:

13 e4??

Earlier in this book I described an error I had made
on the thirteenth move in another game. I still main-
tain that there is absolutely no significance whatso-
ever to the number thirteen. Not a bit. None.

13 . . .   e5!

If now 14 dxe5 d4! 15 Qxd4 fxe5 16 Bxe5 Nxe5 17
Qxe5 Qxd2 and Black wins.

The truth is that I saw 13 . . . e5 coming and
planned to meet it with 14 Be3, but only now discovered that 14 . . . c5! wins a piece anyway. So I tried to
make the best of a bad bargain.

14 exd5	exf4
15 dxc6	bxc6
16 Bxc6	Rb8
17 c5	Qc7
18 Bd5+	Kh8
19 Rfe1	fxg3
20 hxg3	f5?

Black should not take the threat of Bf7 so lightly.
After the careful 20 . . . Nf8, it is doubtful whether
White's connected pawns are worth a piece.

21 Bf7	Bb7
22 Bxe8	Rxe8

Now Black's plan is clear. He wants to attack on the
long diagonal with the help of the strong bishop on

b7, which at the same time blocks my passed pawns. Obviously, he did not count on my reply, turning the tables.

23 c6!!	Qxc6
24 Qxc6	Bxc6
25 Rac1	Nb8

Black's last three moves were all forced. In this endgame my two rooks are stronger than Black's three pieces. For instance, I could win a piece at once with 26 d5, but after 26 ... Bxd5 27 Rxe7 Rxe7 28 Rc8 + Bg8 29 Rxb8 the game looks drawish. With Black's pieces all tied up, I wanted more.

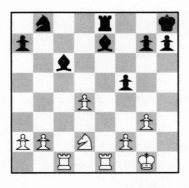

26 Re5!	Kg8
27 d5	Bd7
28 d6!	Bd8

If 28 ... Bxd6 29 Rxe8 + Bxe8 30 Rc8 Kf7 31 Nc4 and wins.

29 Rxe8 +	Bxe8
30 Rc8	Nc6
31 b4	a6

32 a4	Bd7
33 Ra8	Kf7
34 b5	axb5
35 axb5	Bf6
36 b6!?	

It seems rather surprising that after working so hard to win back the piece, White doesn't take it. 36 bxc6 should win too, but it would be easier for Black to defend after that move than after the text, which threatens 37 b7 and Rc8 or Nc4-a5. If 36 . . . Nd8 37 Rxd8 Bxd8 38 b7 wins.

Not taking the piece was a good move psychologically, since my opponent was short of time and I wanted to keep up the pressure with complications.

36 . . .	Be6
37 b7	Be5
38 Rc8!	Na7
39 Rf8 + ?	

Luckily, this rook blunder doesn't change the outcome. 39 Rc7 + ends the game immediately.

The last moves were: 39 . . . Kxf8 40 b8(Q) + Nc8 41 Nc4 Bd4 42 Qb5 Kf7 43 d7 Na7 44 Qb7 Ke7 45 Qc7 Bxd7 46 Qd6 + and Black resigned.

The story of this game has an amusing finish. Soon after it was played, it appeared in various publications accompanied by high praise for the brilliant piece sacrifice on my fourteenth move! Wouldn't it be great if all our blunders turned out to be winning sacrifices?

PSYCHOANALYSIS OF A BLUNDER

Not every blunder is punished, but even if your opponent has let you off the hook, you should not simply breathe a sigh of relief and forget about it. Always analyze your mistakes to find out how and why you made them so that maybe, just maybe, you won't make them again.

For instance, look at the instructive blunder I made in the following position.

NEW YORK OPEN 1990

N. Rogers

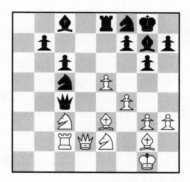

P. Benko

I played 25 Nd5??, and after 25 ... Ne4 26 Rxc4 Nxd2 27 Bxd2 cxd5 28 Bxd5 Bxh3 there was nothing left to fight for, so I accepted my opponent's draw offer.

Only after playing the awful Nd5?? did I realize that 25 Nd1 or 25 Na2 would have won a piece and the game. Even a Class C player would have seen that. So why did I throw away my knight?

Part of the reason was lack of sleep. My previous game was an interesting theoretical endgame in which I had two knights against a pawn. I knew it would be a long endgame and I could have avoided it, but I had never had a chance to play that position before and I wanted to see it through to the end. But the end didn't come until 4 A.M. My game with Rogers started at 10 the same morning.

As explained earlier in this book, it's important to be rested when you sit down for a game. Unfortunately, the scheduling of games in many open tournaments—like this one, in which we had to play two games a day—makes that quite difficult. Insurance company statistics show how sleep deprivation can cause serious automobile and industrial accidents. No wonder it also leads to blunders on the chessboard.

Typically, in the last round of open tournaments the level of play is markedly lower, the number of blunders higher. The reason is not only the increased tension (see Chapter 11, "The Last Round and Other Crises"), but also that many of the players are exhausted after long hours of chess play and insufficient sleep. Lack of rest impairs memory and concentration, which impairs judgment.

In the Rogers game I assumed, without much calculation, that moving my knight aggressively forward was better than the alternatives. It looks like the natural move, doesn't it? I showed the above position to three grandmasters and five masters, and asked each of them what move he would choose. Seven of them picked Nd5?? after a few moments' thought.

That is not so amazing when you think about it. Chess is a vertical game. Pawns move only forward. Our pieces start out at the near end of the board, and we move or aim them toward the enemy king, which is at the far end. We thus have a natural tendency to advance, and so we often do not give due consider-

246

ation to moves that appear to be retreats. Tests have shown that we have little trouble seeing threats on the vertical plane, such as mate on the first rank, but we often miss horizontal threats.

Some players have a tendency to blunder one type of piece with unusual frequency. For me it's the rook. I have blundered away more rooks than all the other pieces combined. I think the reason is that the rooks are not involved in the opening and early middle-game, and after placing them somewhere on the first rank, I tend to forget about them.

Another common type of blunder is to switch the moves of a planned sequence. After calculating a few moves ahead, you check your analysis to make sure you aren't overlooking something. Then you make the second move of the series instead of the first. This is a result of simple anxiety or time pressure.

Even worse is the kind of blunder I made against Fischer at the Candidates' tournament in Curaçao 1962.

P. Benko

R. Fischer

My last move was to put my bishop on a better diagonal by shifting it from e7 to f6. I realized, of course, that my e-pawn was attacked twice and defended only once, but Fischer couldn't take it because of a trap I had worked out.

After making my move, I pressed the clock and got up to visit the restroom. When I returned, I smiled when I saw that Fischer had indeed played 19 Nxe6?, falling into the trap. Unthinkingly, and before even sitting down, I grabbed his knight with 19 . . . Bxe6??, completely forgetting, for that one moment, what I had planned in case he took the poisoned pawn: 19 . . . Bxb2 + ! forces a draw: 20 Kxb2 Qb4 + 21 Kc1 Qa3 + 22 Kd2 Qa5 + 23 Kc1 (*23 Ke3? Bxe6* and Black wins) 23 . . . Qa3 +, etc.

This is just about the most heartbreaking kind of blunder: you've got a good position, your analysis is correct, your opponent has no idea what's coming— and in a single careless moment, you blow it.

Nobody can concentrate at full intensity for five uninterrupted hours. We need to stretch our legs every so often, get some refreshment, rest the brain for a few minutes. Just remember that when you leave the board you break your concentration. When you return, be sure to take a minute or two to get your head on straight. Remember what happened to Pal Benko against Bobby Fischer in Curaçao.

■ ■ ■

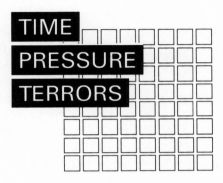

CHAPTER 15

TIME PRESSURE TERRORS

In tournament competition, failure to complete a certain number of moves in a certain amount of time is punishable by death; that is, loss of the game.

Just when the position is reaching critical mass, when every move must be carefully weighed and calculated, when the chessboard demands your entire concentration . . . just then, the clock becomes the center of your life, the sole arbiter of life and death. A disagreeable thought now takes possession of your mind: if you make the time control without ruining your position, you will live; if you don't, you will die.

Flirting with death on the chessboard, even though the king will rise again to fight another day, is an incredibly nerve-racking ordeal. It is not for the faint of heart.

On the other hand, few experiences are as exhilarating as beating the clock with nanoseconds to spare and outplaying your opponent to boot.

Time pressure has been my companion all my chess playing life. In my early days I always managed, despite the most desperate time pressure, to make it safely to the time control without seriously damaging my position. But as I grew older and my reflexes became less dependable, time pressure stopped being fun, and I didn't always make it safely to the time control. I lost many games by overstepping the time limit and many others by rushing my moves to avoid overstepping. The number of winning positions I failed to win is legion.

For example, look at what I did in time pressure against Popov in Reggio Emilia 1970:

L. Popov

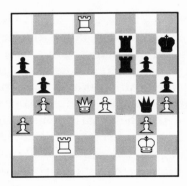

P. Benko

By forcing the exchange of queens and a pair of rooks, I could have gone into an easily won rook-and-pawn endgame. But that would have meant adjourning the game and finishing it another day. I didn't want to do that. We were playing on New Year's Eve, and I had promised myself not to start the new year with an adjourned game.

Considering my serious time pressure, maybe it would have been wiser to trade down and adjourn the game. But there was nothing wrong with what I played: 1 Qxf6!!, a perfectly sound queen sacrifice that Black couldn't accept because of 2 Rc7+ and 3 Rh8 mate. His only move was the spite check 1 . . . Qxe4+.

Without thinking (I had no time to think!), I replied 2 Kh2??, reversing the two moves of my planned continuation, and after 2 . . . Qxc2+ I quit the game in disgust. The right move is 2 Kg1, and after 2 . . . Qe3+ or 2 . . . Qe1+, *now* I play 3 Kh2, and Black can resign.

Did you find that amusing? I didn't. After a few more horrible experiences like that, I began to make a serious effort to use my time more efficiently, but thinking about the clock even when I wasn't in time pressure was too distracting. I finally decided to stop fighting it. A time pressure player I was, and a time pressure player I would always be.

It is some consolation to know that although many other sufferers have tried to cure themselves of their chronic time pressure, no one I know has actually succeeded.

Anyone can get into time pressure now and then due to an unusually complex position or a fast time control or an alarm clock that failed to go off. Chronic time pressure, however, is a psychological problem. It is not merely a bad habit that you can stop, like swearing, but has all the earmarks of an addiction.

As with any addiction, its sufferers come up with all kinds of explanations to avoid doing something about it. Their most common claim is that they play better in time pressure. The urgency of the approaching time control, they say, forces them to concentrate.

I've also heard players say that they get into time pressure on purpose because it upsets their opponents.

Hogwash.

Granted, experienced players can make a high proportion of reasonably good moves in very little time. But common sense tells you that a few seconds aren't enough to work out all the details of a combination or to make sure you're not overlooking some subtle threat. You simply can't play as well when you're short of time as when you have plenty of it.

"When a man knows he is to be hanged in a fortnight," said Samuel Johnson, "it concentrates his mind wonderfully." It is true that as the time control approaches, you stop thinking about food and sex and begin to concentrate wonderfully on the position. But why is it that we don't like to make decisions until we are forced to make them? Wouldn't it make more sense to act more quickly when we aren't rushed so that we aren't rushed later?

Buridan, a fourteenth-century philosopher, is said to have been the creator of this famous model of indecision: If an ass stood between two haystacks that were equidistant from him and were in every way equal, he would starve to death, having no reason to choose one over the other.

Chess players, like Buridan's ass, can often find no compelling reason to choose one move or variation over others that appear to him equally good. It's usually impossible to calculate a variation all the way to mate, yet we worry that we haven't looked deeply enough, that we aren't seeing everything. We're afraid that if we choose this path, we'll regret not having chosen that one. So we put off the decision, waiting for a little bird to whisper, "Make *that* move."

If you've ever listened to chess players talk about the games they've lost, you've certainly heard somebody offer the excuse that his mistake was caused by time pressure. In reality, his mistake was that he allowed himself to be the victim of time pressure.

Alekhine wrote somewhere that a player who blames his bad play on time pressure is like a criminal whose alibi is that he was drunk when he committed the crime. The ability to manage time, said Alekhine, is just as important as the ability to play endgames.

Still, if the game is important enough or complicated enough, or both, even the greatest players can fall victim to time-pressure blindness.

In the following position, from the fifth game of the 1978 World Championship Match, challenger Viktor Korchnoi had an outright win.

A. Karpov

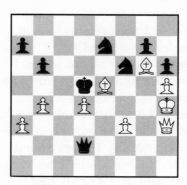

V. Korchnoi

Both players were in desperate time pressure and could think only about reaching the time control at move fifty-six. With two moves to go, Korchnoi played the blunder 55 Be4 + ?? and the game was drawn after a marathon endgame. With 55 Bf7 + , Korchnoi would have won quickly: 55 . . . Kc6 56 Qe6 + and mate in a few moves.

Maybe it's too late for you, as it is for me, to learn to make decisions more quickly so that you don't get into time pressure. But if you think you can learn to manage your time better, do it now. If you wait until you've started making excuses, it may be too late.

WHAT TO DO ABOUT TIME PRESSURE (YOURS)

All right, let's say you're a chronic, incurable time-pressure player. Here are a few tips from someone who knows what it's like.

The most dangerous (some would say the most exciting) situation is to be both in time pressure and in a complicated tactical melee at the same time. Here is Dr. Benko's prescription: Avoid time pressure. If you're already *in* time pressure, avoid tactical complications. Repeat as needed.

Smyslov provided an object lesson in a game we played many years ago. In a promising position just after the opening, I spent forty-five minutes working out a complicated line that would have been dangerous for him if he made the move I was hoping for. His reply came as a shock. It was sound and simple, avoided all the complications I had spent so much time analyzing, and, worst of all, had taken him all of two minutes to find! The result: I was far behind on the clock with nothing to show for all that heavy thinking.

I asked Smyslov after the game whether he saw my variation. He never considered it, he said, because he knew the time I had spent on that one move would later prove costly. Why risk going into a line that I knew much better than he did, especially when he already had a clear advantage in time at no cost to himself?

He was right, of course. Although I had winning chances later in the game, my time pressure made it impossible for me to cash in my positional advantage and I had to offer a draw.

Grandmaster Arthur Bisguier, a practical and realistic player, also showed good sense in a game against Fischer in a United States Championship in the 1960s. In the early middlegame, Fischer, as White in a Ruy Lopez, played his knight to d5, sacrificing a pawn. Bisguier declined the sacrifice after only a minute's thought—hardly long enough to have considered all the ramifications of accepting it.

Why did Bisguier reply so quickly? Because, he answered, "Fischer does not make unsound sacrifices. I wasn't going to waste half an hour on the clock to prove to myself that I couldn't take the pawn. I already knew that."

You can't avoid complications all the time, but you can try. As we advised in an earlier chapter, choose an opening repertoire that is suited to your natural style. If you dislike tactical situations in the late middlegame (that is, when time pressure is most likely to occur), don't play 1 e4 against Sicilian players or 1 d4 against people who like the King's Indian or the Slav Defense. As Black, you should avoid those same openings.

Don't make far-reaching plans when you're in time pressure. If you calculate a long variation and your opponent doesn't play what you expected, you won't have the time to work out the best response. Play simple, clear, natural moves.

It's often a good idea to release the tension by exchanging pawns or to eliminate certain dangers by trading queens or other pieces. Of course, you'll have to evaluate the possible endgame before making any such irrevocable decision, but that's something you should think about long before time pressure arrives.

It's important to remember that you can't win games by running away every time your opponent makes a fist. You have to fight. Tactics, complications, sacrifices—all belong to our game of chess.

If you are weak or insecure in tactics, play lots of speed games with your friends and practice playing gambit openings against your computer. Don't worry about winning; just learn to see and to calculate. Improvement will come.

Then go ahead and play the Sicilian and the Slav and let your *opponents* worry about the complications.

WHAT TO DO ABOUT TIME PRESSURE (YOUR OPPONENT'S)

What's the best way to play when your opponent is in time pressure and you aren't?

If you move slowly, you help your opponent by letting him think on your time. If you try to rush him by moving quickly, you deprive him of that extra time but artificially create time pressure for yourself.

The first alternative makes the most sense. Speaking for myself, as one who has been in time pressure once or twice, what makes me most uncomfortable is having to sit alertly at the board for long minutes, waiting anxiously for my opponent to move so that I can reply without delay. I dare not get up even for a drink of water.

And having no productive thinking of my own to do

increases my impatience and affects my concentration. Usually, I've already planned how I will continue. A long wait can make me forget some of my prepared moves or get them mixed up.

I think the best idea is to plan a series of moves, play them fairly quickly, and then stop for a while to plan the next series. Of course, you will have to be ready to abandon that plan if your opponent plays something you weren't expecting.

Trying to rush a player in time pressure is bad strategy and bad psychology. Nothing is to be gained by creating time pressure for yourself, and everything is to be lost if your time shortage causes you to blunder. It's tempting to keep up with your opponent's nervous tempo, but don't let yourself be pushed into a game of speed chess. That helps only your opponent.

On the other hand, if you have a lost position, you may as well try speed chess—you can only lose a game once. Maybe your opponent will get rattled and blow his advantage. Remember: what counts is the point, not how you got it (or lost it).

Under no circumstances should you play fast if you have a winning position. Forget the clock. Use all your time and make good moves. The one thing a player dreads most when he's under time pressure is seeing his opponent calmly making strong moves.

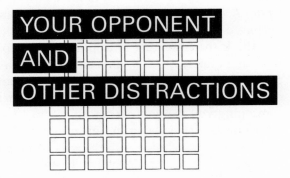

CHAPTER 16

YOUR OPPONENT AND OTHER DISTRACTIONS

The lapwing (or pewit), a member of the plover family, is a brightly colored bird known for its erratic flight and irritating cry. The German word for this obnoxious fellow is *Kiebitz*, a word which the Germans use appropriately to describe a similarly obnoxious person; that is, a busybody. The verb form, *kiebitzen*, means "to look over the shoulder of a card player"—that is, to kibitz.

In Yiddish, a form of German, the verb *kibitz* and the noun *kibitzer*, which have both been absorbed into the English language, refer not to a variety of bird but to, among other things, a variety of nuisance. The variety of nuisance that hangs around people when they're playing chess or card games.

Kibitzers don't play; they kibitz. They always know what you should have played, and they will tell you without being asked. They will tell you if they are asked *not* to. Sometimes, they will even tell you what you should play before you play it. During casual games in a chess club or in the park, this is merely annoying. In a tournament, it's annoying and against the rules.

But the thing about kibitzers is that it's almost impossible to shut them up, rules or no rules. For example, a game between Drew and Thompson in the 1938 British Ladies Championship was adjourned in the following position with Black to seal her move.

Thompson

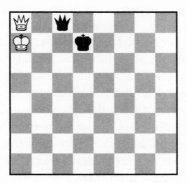

Drew

Mrs. Thompson sealed the best move, 1 . . . Qc5+. But several spectators thought the position was drawn, and they communicated their opinion to Mrs. Thompson, who informed Miss Drew that she would be satisfied with a draw. And so it was recorded.

But 1 . . . Qc5+ leads to a forced mate: 2 Ka6 Qa3+ 3 Kb7 Qb4+ 4 Ka6 Qa4+ 5 Kb7 Qb5+ 6 Ka7 Kc7, etc.

Probably that was the last time Mrs. Thompson took advice from a spectator. And let it be a lesson to you, too, dear reader.

Kibitzers—i.e., nonparticipants—are not the worst distracters. The worst distracters are other participants—i.e., your opponents. They fidget and stare and scratch and hum and drum their fingers and tap their feet and suck their teeth and adjust the pieces and pace the floor and stand behind you.

Some players do these or other things deliberately to annoy you. Such practices are, at best, unethical. Do not indulge in them. Chess players inhabit a rather small world, and you do not want to earn a reputation as an unethical player. Like "J'adoubovic."

Formal chess is played with the touch-move rule: if you touch a piece, you must move it. But if you merely want to center it in its square, you are supposed to alert your opponent to your intention by saying, in advance, "J'adoube" or "I adjust" or some similar phrase.

The behavior of Grandmaster Milan Matulovic of Yugoslavia during his game with Bilek at the 1967 Interzonal in Tunisia stands as one of the most outrageous violations of tournament rules ever perpetrated at an event of such importance. Matulovic moved his bishop, pressed his clock, and suddenly saw that he had made a mistake. So he took back his move, made a different move, and only then said "J'adoube." Bilek jumped up in protest, of course. "But I said j'adoube!" Matulovic exclaimed. A big argument ensued, during which the tournament director, having only Bilek's word to go on, refused to require Matulovic to make a move with his bishop, as the rules provided. Although Matulovic never denied taking his move back, the tournament appeals committee, amazingly, refused to punish him. The game ended in a draw.

Until that game, all the Yugoslav players custom-
arily took their evening meals together in the hotel,
but thenceforth Matulovic dined alone, shunned by
his own compatriots. And ever since that incident, he
has been sneeringly referred to as "J'adoubovic."

A final note of poetic justice: A few days after his
game with Bilek, Matulovic choked on a bone during
dinner and had to be taken to a doctor. From then on,
the joke of the tournament was that the doctor
couldn't find a bone but the word "j'adoube" stuck in
Matulovic's throat.

There are players who nervously center each piece
precisely on its square every chance they get, and
some of them are so compulsive about it that they do
it even while their opponent is thinking. During our
game in the 1971 United States Championship, An-
thony Saidy adjusted the pieces while it was my turn
to move, so I adjusted the pieces when it was *his* turn
to move. Then he did it, then I did it. We soon tired of
our little game and went back to chess. You can't let
them get away with stuff like that.

World Champion Petrosian had the nervous habit
of jiggling his legs under the table, sometimes acci-
dentally kicking his opponent. Petrosian always
claimed he didn't even know he was doing it. Korchnoi, while playing a match with Petrosian, got so upset that, to avoid a fist-fight between these personal
and professional enemies, the match directors had to
install a wooden barrier between them under the
table.

Petrosian, by the way, always wore a hearing aid,
which he turned off while he was playing. His Candidates' match with Robert Hübner in 1971 was played
in a room just below street level. The street noise was
so intolerable to the German grandmaster that he re-

261

signed the match rather than endure it. Petrosian never even heard it.

Tal tries to unnerve his opponents by staring at them while they're thinking, and those large, wild-looking eyes of his seem capable of frying you in your chair. The amazing games he played early in his career led some reporters to suggest that this "devil from Riga" was hypnotizing his opponents.

When I sat down to play him in the Candidates' tournament in Bled 1959, I was wearing dark sunglasses. But although that story has been told in many books and articles over the years, nobody has ever explained it correctly. I wore the glasses not to "ward off" Tal's "evil eye," as has been often said, but as a stunt. A couple of reporters had asked me to put them on to provide an eye-catching photo and a lively story for their newspapers.

Another sort of "staring" took place in a United States Championship game between John Grefe and Kim Commons. Grefe, a follower of the religious leader Mahara Ji, always wore a large button bearing the likeness of the smiling guru. Some of Grefe's opponents had complained about having to look at that face for five hours, but there was nothing the tournament director could do. Commons had the answer. Getting permission to display a button depicting his own hero, Commons sat down to play Grefe wearing a huge smiling picture of . . . Kim Commons.

What should you do if your opponent or anyone else is distracting you, deliberately or not? What you should *not* do is try to get him to stop. That could provoke an argument which would only get you more upset. The thing to do is to complain directly to the tournament director. He has the duty and the authority to do something about it. Your job is to keep your mind on the game.

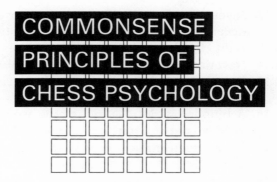

CHAPTER 17

COMMONSENSE PRINCIPLES OF CHESS PSYCHOLOGY

1. Know yourself.
2. Know your opponent.
3. Be patient.
4. Avoid overconfidence.
5. Be prepared to fight. Your opponent will be.
6. Keep your mind on the game and your behind on the chair.
7. Respect every opponent—male, female, child, or computer—but beat him, her, or it anyway.
8. If it's good for your opponent, it's bad for you; if it's good for you, it's bad for your opponent.
9. Find your natural style and don't fight it.
10. Analyze, don't guess. The battlefield is littered with fallen kings whose dying words were, "I didn't see that."
11. Be realistic. Don't attack when your position doesn't justify attacking, and don't defend against imagined threats.

■ ■ ■ ■ ■

12. Play openings that force your opponent out of his natural style.

13. If your opponent plays an opening move you've never seen before, don't waste time trying to refute it. Play sound developing moves.

14. Never offer a draw unless you really want one.

15. You can't win by resigning, and you can't win by agreeing to draws.

16. A blunder is not the end of the world. Keep your wits about you. It ain't over till it's over.

17. If you are losing, sell your life as dearly as possible.

18. The ability to manage time is as important as the ability to play endgames (Alekhine).

19. When in time pressure, avoid complications. If you can't avoid complications, avoid time pressure.

20. Rushing your opponent when he's in time pressure by moving quickly creates artificial time pressure for yourself.

21. If your concentration is broken, don't make your next move until you've studied the position and are sure you know what's going on.

22. Arrive for your games on time. If your opponent is late, it's his problem; don't make it yours by trying to take advantage of it.

23. Get plenty of rest, watch what you eat, keep fit.

24. Psychology is a powerful weapon, but it is not a substitute for knowledge, imagination, and technique.

■ ■ ■